The Girl Who Spoke with Giants

A Novel

Christopher Noël

Also by the author

*The Mind of Sasquatch and the Secret to Their Success
(a theory)*

*Our Life with Bigfoot:
Knowing Our Next of Kin at Habituation Sites*

*How Sasquatch Matters:
Writers Respond to the New Natural Order* (anthology)

*Sasquatch Rising 2013: How DNA Breakthroughs and
Backyard Visits Reveal the Greatest Story of Our Time*

Doctor White's Monkey (stories)

*In the Unlikely Event of a Water Landing:
A Geography of Grief* (memoir)

Hazard and the Five Delights (novel)

Thanks to the Isabel Circle Refuge and to that corner conversation.

A tree falls. All night long, my wind's been shrieking at my bedroom window. Telling me to get ready. The earth shakes. I laugh! I wasn't ready for *that*. I laugh!

Great White is not laughing, not even once. He bangs through the front door and calls out, "Holy…*wow!*"

Out my window, I can see his flashlight whipping back and forth across the goat-house and my blue pool and the water inside my blue pool and the apple tree and the edge of the woods. Till a new wall lights up. Black. A new wall in the world! Reaching roots toward the sky.

By morning, she's still laughing her head off—the head that's ruined my life but pays the bills. And is soon to pay a whole lot better.

At least the damn thing didn't crush the house. It was tall enough but fell instead along the tree line, forming a barrier. Hey, maybe that will keep her from wandering into the wood so much—*don't bet on it*. Tomboy.

I let the goats out. They bounce up to the rootball and start chewing on the mud and pebbles. Idiots.

Pam wants to play with them, on all fours, bouncing too, in her shorts and t-shirt. When she runs on all fours, it's not hands and knees but hands and *feet*. I go inside to get our stuff ready. Call the venue to confirm.

Back outside, I find her standing on top of the fallen tree, arms raised, sneakers probably at my shoulder height. Knees a bloody mess from climbing up the bark.

I'd say screw it except we have a show to do.

In the car, she performs her usual routine, babbling inside jokes with the passing scenery, cackling, wildly flapping her hands and walloping her head every time we pass a horse.

Thank you, Social Media Marketing podcast. I turn up the volume.

We're booked for a middle school assembly, which is a lousy payday, hundred bucks, but hey, we're still nailing down the new tricks. I saw this guy on Jimmy Fallon do the *Rainman* stunt—instantly counting a pile of dropped matches—so we've been practicing and I think she's ready. *Better be.*

Riding in the car, I watch him using the controls. Great White doesn't know how much I watch. I bet I could drive, too.

He gives me pads to press the blood on my knees, which is so hilarious because these are the same ones I use for my personal blood. I try to show him why, but he twists up his face. So hilarious.

I stick my head out the window. My wind is right there to greet me.

"Okay, students and staff, let's all focus now and show some respect for our guests. Today we're proud to welcome—quiet, please—Mr. James Manchester and his daughter, Pamela."

The principal pats Pam's shoulder and of course she slaps his hand away and crouches into a ball on stage. Some kids in the audience laugh and she laughs back, a barking type of laugh, not to mock them but because she copies—that's what she *does*. Annoying as hell but it always goes over at shows. Her laughing makes other kids laugh, and back and forth for a while until the principal finally goes from tapping the microphone to smacking it.

"Now, like some of our fellow students in Miss Tollefson's group, Pamela has a condition known as *autism*. But as we are about to learn, this young lady's affliction comes along with certain abilities."

"We call them *gifts*." I step in and take the mic, which is a moment I love. "Before we proceed, may I ask for a volunteer from way back at the back up there to go to the art room and select a painting or drawing?" Hands shoot up and I pick a blond boy. "Make sure it's one with plenty of detail and please bring it back here, but do not...repeat do *not* come up front with it or show it to my daughter until I give the word."

The blond boy looks at his teacher, she nods, then he dashes out the wide auditorium door.

"While we wait for our friend to return, Pamela would like to show you her first amazing feat." She's rocking on the floor and I know the audience doubts she would like to show them anything, but I say it again, "amazing feat," and she stands up, ready to work. Or at least *willing*. By now, she's learned never to screw up the act.

I pull her sketch pad and marker from my shoulder bag and then our jumbo box of matches.

"Principal Wagner, I'd like to invite you to remove a handful of these matches and drop them right on the floor." He does so.

After about five seconds, Pam's marker squeaks on the paper but she doesn't show the audience what she's written. And she won't speak the number, either. She can't talk unless she's copying someone...or spouting science facts.

"And now," I say to the principal, "please go ahead and count them." From my bag I take a silver plate for him to set each match on. That's a nice touch. I hold the microphone in front of his face.

Pam sways back and forth, clutching the sketch pad to her chest.

"Thirty-eight...thirty-nine..."

I notice the boy returning with the framed picture. I give him a thumbs-up, then push my palm out toward him—sit tight. He shows the picture around just to his friends.

"Eighty-two...eighty-three."

For the last fifteen, I encourage the crowd to join in, so everyone is counting "hundred forty-four...hundred forty-five...hundred forty-six..."

Between two fingers, the principal raises the final match. When I nod at my daughter, she turns her sketch pad around, showing **147**.

The crowd goes wild.

While they're simmering back down, Pam turns to a new, blank page and sits down cross-legged on the stage planks, hunching over her pad with the marker gripped in her fist.

I direct my voice to the back of the auditorium. "At this time, young man, when I say the word, I would like to ask you to turn the art work around but—and this is important—only for *one second*. Understand? Ready? Darling, are you ready, too?"

"Darling ready too," Pam says. Kids laugh nervously. Her voice always sounds like a recording of some real voice inside her that I haven't heard in years and may never hear again.

"Perfect. Okay...show the painting! One thousand one. That's enough!"

Honestly, I could barely make it out—probably two hundred feet away and no wider than the boy's shoulders—except to notice that it's a very realistic drawing of an old-fashioned train. Maybe it's a tracing of a photograph.

The room grows quiet as Pam's marker starts squeaking away.

She sticks her tongue out sideways to concentrate.

"While she's busy, let me briefly explain a bit about my daughter's special condition...bla bla bla...." No, I don't actually *say* the bla bla parts. My brain goes on automatic, and I try not to listen to my own spiel. "Autism afflicts one out of every sixty-eight children in our country...bla...experts not sure what causes it...bla...a variety of forms such as...bla bla...but only ten percent of these children are lucky enough to have what the scientists call *savant* skills. These include mental abilities far beyond those of normal human beings. In the case of my child here, you are about to witness what is known as a *photographic memory*. Ready, Sweetheart?"

Pam stands and holds up her drawing. She shouts "Ready Sweetheart!" and angles the page back and forth—it took me forever to drill that one in: smooth motion—so that everyone can get a good look. The crowd applauds all the details she was able to capture in just three or four minutes, but that's nothing compared to the reaction when I have the boy come forward and climb on stage with us. Now the two kids stand side by side, displaying identical images.

In the goat-house, they press around me in the dark, pushing my back with their flat foreheads and some sharp horns.

At that school, he wouldn't let me run to the car after the show. I had to run because all those eyes shattered me. I had to go into my ball and find the Single Thing again. But he yanked me up. Twisting and burning my wrist.

That teacher stopped Great White and told him things. I couldn't listen even when she tried to speak all soft to me. Everywhere, the eyes kept jabbing at me, wanting me in pieces.

Littler and littler pieces. Hoping I'd explode now and now and now. Or how about now? Shattering me. I tried to get back down onto the floor. To my ball. Great White wouldn't let me.

My wrist still hurts. The nanny goat sniffs it but won't lick.

He used to catch me in the city pool. When I was very little. Before all the eyes tried shattering me. We'd play "shark." He'd pretend to be a great white shark and swim under water. Grab my ankle! That was fun!

"Miss Tollefson had some extremely good news for us. That lady's got connections!" We were riding the car.

I said, "So...the Clark's nutcracker, a type of crow, buries as many as thirty thousand pine seeds in the fall in two hundred square acres and then finds 90% of them in the winter."

"Pam, I know you can understand me. Miss Tollefson is going to help your *career*."

"So...the Clark's nutcracker, a type of crow, buries as many as..."

I'm starving. I drink from the nanny goat. She is going to have babies soon! The milk feels so warm in my belly. In the corner, I rock myself. The rhythm keeps me safe. I go into my ball. Then, the goats press around me again, all five of them with their flat foreheads against my back and some sharp horns.

My wind blows against the outside walls. There are no windows in the goat-house so I'm extra safe. My wind makes a moaning sound that cares about me. It is a good friend. I love the flat foreheads pushing my back. Pushing me back together into one piece. Tomorrow I will visit the Single Thing up on the ridge.

I find her where I know she'll be and since it's not a cold night—still summertime, though tipping into fall—I just leave her there. I got her an old mattress once but she likes the hard floor. Once, I snuck inside with a blanket, but the goats went ballistic—idiots—and then of course she started screaming too.

Besides, I am very busy on Facebook tonight, considering new offers, setting up shows for the upcoming days and weeks. The video of yesterday's performance has already gotten seven hundred views and sixty-two likes. Okay…not quite viral, but Tollefson is pure gold. Spreading the word. Should pay her ten percent…*ha!*

I've been hoping—*knowing*—that such a moment would come along at one of these pathetic little venues. It's called paying your dues so that when the break finally comes along, you're ready. You deserve it.

She was waving around a video camera and asking permission to post our show on YouTube and Facebook. Like I'm going to say no, especially after she told me she's President of the National bla Alliance on Autistic bla bla. Pumping my arm, she goes, "Your daughter's gifts will inspire millions of families, and teach our young people on the spectrum how to unlock their own blablabla."

Around her was a flock of *special* students, some spazzing out, mumbling to themselves, hopping up and down, drooling. Many ages but one girl was in like kindergarten, reminding me of when Helen and I first took Pam to a shrink and got our diagnosis. Probably waited too long—she was nearly five—but for the record she'd been perfectly normal up to the age of three. Well, *pretty* normal, just a few symptoms to start with, rocking and swaying. But she *interacted* with us, complete with eye contact, so we were happy. She'd smile at us and actually talk to us and ask questions and answer our questions. No, "You didn't do anything wrong," Doctor Stevens assured us.

When Pam started falling away and acting all spooky, it was so gradual at first that Helen and I could ignore the problem. But spazzing out came next—wildly flapping her hands beside her ears, walloping her own head, cackling or shrieking at nothing, talking in long streams of gibberish. She'd no longer look at us and whenever we'd dare to look her in the eyes, she'd throw tantrums. If we got too close, she'd scratch us.

Marlene Stevens explained that profoundly autistic children lose the ability to communicate with others directly, because "direct contact causes them extreme trauma, what we call *exposure anxiety.*" They cannot bear to reveal their true inner selves. The outside world, and especially other people, represent chaos and danger, so the autistic child must fight back with distance and coping methods like repetitive behaviors and intensive rituals that shut the world out and create structure. "The challenge," she told us, "is to find *indirect* modes of social interaction."

So we set up dates with other autistic kids and let them engage in "parallel play"—what a freak show that was.

This morning, I find my little bundle of joy still in the goat-house, on her hands and knees drinking from the nanny. That's right, suckling like a baby goat. Breakfast. This behavior makes me sick but it has never made *her* sick. In fact, it calms her way down. Saves me work, too—I'm a business man, not a farmer—but I can't watch. I shut the goat-house door.

She's allergic to cow's milk, and many other foods, which is why we had to get these stinking idiots in the first place, back when Helen still lived with us, before she jumped ship. Joke's on her now. She'll probably come crawling back here once she sees us on Jimmy Fallon.

Pam's been in training for two years and now she'll finally get the chance to make me proud. And buy us a brand new car. Or hell...an RV covered with signs—**KID GENIUS! YOU WON'T BELIEVE YOUR EYES! FEATS OF MENTAL MAGIC! WORLD FAMOUS!!!**

Great White tip-toes around. Staying away so I won't bolt or ball up or shriek in his ear or tell him science. He understands not to look in my eyes or talk to me if he wants me to pay attention. He understands not to pay attention to *me*.

Sometimes, he'll stand across the back yard and explain his ideas to the apple tree, and if I'm in the right mood, I might listen. For a new trick he wants me to learn, he'll set up the stage in the yard and pretend the apple tree is me and teach it the new trick again and again. I will learn it from a distance out the corner of my ear. Then, I will stop listening and go back to Minecraft on my Kindle. Over there, he'll keep teaching the tree and teaching the tree, like I didn't get it the first time.

When it's time for me to practice for a show, if I'm not in the mood, I'll pretend not to know the trick and pretend not to be pretending. I'm really good at pretending both. Great White will get so mad and I will laugh. I'll laugh!

Right now, he's standing at the goat-house door, way too excited about some "big break." His mouth is barking about "likes," "views," some video, a new car, and the "next level." Like levels of ore in Minecraft?

I smack my hands over my ears and yell, "So…the blue whale is the largest creature that has ever lived on Earth. It weighs the same as twenty-two elephants. Its heart is the size of a small car, and its largest blood vessels are wide enough for a human being to swim through without much difficulty."

He waits till I slide my hands off my ears, then says, "All I know is you better be on your best game, Little Ticket."

But I am already back to fighting off monsters.

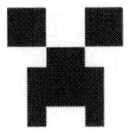

It wasn't too long after Helen left that I started to crack the code. Ironic, I'd say. We'd been trying to reach Pam face to face, and that sure didn't work—she'd only slap us or shriek in our faces like we were trying to murder her.

Because of our daughter's allergies, Helen used to make her these miniature whole wheat muffins, which were disgusting, but which Pam loved. If we made the mistake of addressing her directly, she'd scream and pitch them across the room at us. She had amazing aim even then. This was just about the only thing my wife and I could agree on—kid was accurate with a muffin. She could hit the same spot on the kitchen door, again and again, from her seat at the table twenty feet away—and I mean the *same spot*. She'd do it every time I used her name. "Pam!" *Bang.* "Pam!" *Bang.* Though it was a waste of food and kind of alarming, Helen and I had to laugh and look at each other with congratulations in our eyes for what we had created. She even joked about taking Pam on the road, selling tickets, finally finding a benefit in our long nightmare.

I thought...*Hey.*

But those moments were not common. Basically, the more we failed to reach our daughter, the more spastic meltdowns she threw, the more my wife and I hated each other. And then, once I didn't have Helen around anymore, I could concentrate on solving the strange little puzzle before me. At that point, it was basically sink or swim for my girl and me.

Speaking of which, I couldn't take her to the city pool anymore and play our shark game. She couldn't handle the public. Even if they'd suddenly disappeared, she probably wouldn't have been able to handle the shark.

One day, I got so frustrated I stopped talking to her completely and started talking to her Dora the Explorer doll instead. A guy's got to have company. And I thought, *maybe it'll make her jealous...or something.*

So Pam's way down the hall in her room, clanging on the walls with a milking bucket, and I start telling Dora about my childhood bike accident, where I broke my leg. All the gory details.

Now get this. That milking bucket never stopped banging through the whole story, but later that afternoon, many hours later, Pam was back in the living room finally tuckered out and watching cartoons on TV. And right out of the blue she goes, "Broke my leg in two places...half an inch from a major artery."

I almost ran over and hugged her and threw her up into the air, but I held myself back. Enough scars on my arms and face already.

Seven years later and she's pretty much an open book to me now. You've just got to play the angles and work around her wild times. I'm gradually taming her. Hey, it's not rocket science. On the other hand, it *is* a kind of brain surgery.

The new path up to the ridge is 1565 steps, starting from the wall of roots. My wind pulled the tree down for me, so I gather pebbles from the wall and fill my pockets, then march uphill. It is very strange not to use my old path, which is only 1498 steps and all worn down. My feet know every root. The new path trips me five times, tears open the scabs on my knees.

My spot is a soft meadow. There's plenty of room to work on the Single Thing. I take the pebbles from my pockets and add them on. The nose looks better already.

The Single Thing is a head that comes up to my shoulder. Exactly how high I planned it. It's made of dried mud and stones. For the face, twigs and leaves and little pebbles. I ran out of driveway pebbles long ago. That's why the tree fell.

We leave the rest of the world behind, the Single Thing and I. I sit with my back against it. It keeps me company.

Great White never puts one toe into these woods. No. Every time he watches me disappearing in here, he stays put on the yard or behind a window. Usually behind the kitchen window, with his coffee cup. Poor scared Great White.

Ha! I'm breaking into the nationwide autism network from the comfort of my own home. The video of our assembly performance has blown up, hitting hit 6050 views on YouTube by ten o'clock this morning. And the invitations are streaming in I'm talking professional level now. Managing her career used to be too hard—now it's too easy! The most attractive offer so far is a conference in Kansas City—Institute for Cognitive bla bla— but it's last minute, next *Wednesday*. They're going to pay air fare plus $900. Yes, please. Book it!

Now I'm just trying to picture Pam on a plane.

"You need to listen up for once, Little Ticket."

I'm splashing in the blue pool. Splashing the water up in front of my eyes so sunlight sparkles through. It plays a thousand different games with my eyes. Making jokes. Stars. Stars and jokes. Stars and jokes!

Sixty-seven splashes…sixty-eight…sixty-nine…

We got this little blue pool for the yard after we stopped going to the city pool.

"You need to stop that and listen to me now, Pam. This is very important. We're going to Kansas City!"

Seventy-five…seventy-six…

He taught the new trick to the apple tree for five days in a row. He needs to leave me alone because I am very, very busy.

Eight-two…eighty-three….eighty-four…

But I have to leave the blue pool. He's getting way too close. I run and hide behind the fallen tree. His words are far away now. Under a flat rock, I find a colony of ants. They are busy with *their* work, too. They are light red. I love the patterns they make when I look at them all at once. I love to watch them carry their pale eggs to their tunnels and down underground. Their eggs are in danger because of me. Hold them in our jaws! Time to get them underground!

So…the role of reproduction is to provide for the continued existence of a species. It is the process by which living organisms duplicate themselves.

"Pam!"

Every time he says my name it's like a punch in the face.

"I know you're paying attention in there. I know you way better than you think I do. Listen, our next show is the day after tomorrow and it will be longer than any we've done before, so we need to rehearse the thumbprint trick."

"So…" I shout, "ant societies have division of labor, communication between individuals, and the ability to solve complex problems. They are the world's strongest creatures in relation to their size. The total weight of ants on Earth equals the total weight of people."

I hear him pacing back and forth out on the grass.

"I know, right?" he says. "Pretty amazing, I agree. I once heard that an ant can lift one hundred times its body weight. Wouldn't that be great if we could do that? I could probably lift our *car* over my head. And I bet you could..."

But I am silently crawling away up the slope, using my antenna to taste the air. Mushrooms. Worms. He can't see me so he just keeps trying to tell *me* science. Hilarious. So hilarious!

He rattles the papers in his hand. The ones with all the black thumbprints on them.

"Pam! I've been pretty easy on you up till now, but that ends today, do you hear me? Your career is about to take off for real and you will need to start being a lot more *professional* about it."

When he taught the apple tree the thumbprint trick, he used the goats as an audience. He always pretends not to hate them when he's teaching. Like I don't know the difference. "Ladies and gentlemen, I am going to ask for volunteers to come up here on stage, press your thumbs into the ink, and leave your prints on this paper for my daughter to memorize." The goats said *mehhhhhh!* "So many hands! Okay, don't worry, folks, this girl's brain power has no limitations. Just line up over there..."

After checking for me behind the tree, he explodes, but I'm already at the top of the first hill. I hear his voice but not his words anymore. My wind sails them away.

There are light red ants on my knees, exploring my scabs, which are starting to grow back. My scabs are light red too. I have to find out if ants can tell color. They are tickling the skin around the edges of the scabs but not biting.

Great White is in the woods! I smack my hands onto my mouth. So I won't scream. I hear the papers landing on old dead leaves, and his footsteps snapping twigs here and there down below me. He doesn't know where I've gone.

I scoot behind a thick tree so he double doesn't know where I am. How can I triple it?

But it goes to zero when he charges up the hill toward me. I must have made a sound. That's one part I can't always control. My quick sounds.

I get up and run. I can't believe he is in the woods for the first time. I run faster. I picture the light red ants riding the scabs. Trying to hang on. Maybe from bending, the scabs will crack open and the ants can hang onto the cracks.

"I swear I'm gonna take more control around here. This isn't some game anymore, this is...real life. Time...to...wake..."

He's out of breath already. I would never lead him to my spot and the Single Thing. I go in a very different direction.

What's this? A t-pee of pine branches to hide in. Somebody made this t-pee for me. With my antenna, I can still taste the sweet smell of the broken branches. The sweet smell comes out when you break a living pine branch. I have done this so many times just for the smell. I never built anything with the branches. I've been too busy building the Single Thing and making it look just right. I should build one of these t-pees, too. They let you feel invisible, with all the needles for walls. Some soft branches cover the floor, too.

I sit inside it. Check my scabs. One *has* cracked from bending, but the ants all fell off.

Great White is stepping slowly down below, listening for another mistake. Again, I clamp my hands over my mouth. Now all my breathing is the sweet kind.

Here in my new house, I snap pictures with my eyes. click click click click. In the shadows...a surprise.

The sound of stones clacking together finally gives away her location—*ha!*

But the first impact stops me cold, maybe three feet from my head and right at eye level, the rock bouncing off a tree and rolling at my feet.

At the top of the hill, backlit light as in a horror movie, my devil daughter stands with another round rock in her hand. She doesn't look directly at me, of course, but her next throw is a line drive that sounds like a bomb against the tree just inches from my ear.

She's graduated from whole wheat muffins.

I turn and escape these damn woods. I'm obviously no match for her up in there. But luckily, I've made myself ready for this day—the day she'd finally leave me no other choice.

Following my Action Plan, I grab the bottle from my medicine cabinet, then prepare the paste in a bowl—a mixture of water and ketamine hydrochloride (powder form, tasteless)—and then carry it to the goat-house. There's only one nanny who's pregnant with an udder full of milk. All five idiots scream at me while I quickly apply the thin paste to her teats.

Now I can just sit back and watch at my leisure from my office window, while firming up the details of our trip.

Hey, I have to get her to Kansas City somehow, don't I? We'll arrive a day early so we can rehearse in the hotel room.

She'll be fine...and certainly thank me in near future, when we're rich and famous.

■

"Ladies and gentlemen, it gives me great pleasure this morning to introduce you to our very special guests, James Manchester and his daughter, Pamela Manchester. When you witness her abilities, I think you will agree..."

I stop listening to the man's voice. I am still inside the t-pee in the woods. Smelling the sweet, sweet pine. Till Great White yanks my wrist hard and I have to open my eyes.

"...she may help to advance our understanding of Savant Syndrome and its idiopathic cognitive bla bla."

The conference chairman ushers us to the stage. At least Pam is walking again, though the polite applause causes her obvious pain. She clamps her hands over her ears.

But honestly, she looks quite presentable. I gave her a shower and crammed her into a yellow dress she's never worn before. It sort of fits, even though I don't technically know her size. That's what mothers are for. I brushed her hair and even found a red ribbon to tie it back with.

I make my usual introductory remarks and then we swing right into the matchbox trick. I want to take Pam's mind off everything but her work. Let me say it's a huge relief when the audience and the chairman count up to two hundred and eleven matches, and of course that is exactly what Pam has written—shakily this time—on her sketch pad.

The crowd doesn't go wild, because they are in the brain bizz and they all know the famous match-counting scene from *Rainman*.

Pam sits down and starts picking at a scab on her knee. Crap like that won't fly on Jimmy Fallon, but lucky for me this is a room full of career psychologists—a tough crowd to gross out.

This has *not* been a good time for us. Yesterday, she woke up suddenly at thirty-five thousand feet and went ballistic, screaming up and down the aisle, impossible to restrain and nearly forcing the plane to land in freakin' Des Moines. Then, just as suddenly, she did her roll-up-and-freeze routine. I had to carry her like a boulder through the airport—thank God for the people-mover sidewalks, which gave me a break, although she'd kind of roll off the ends—then to our rental car where I dumped her in the back seat.

"Next, folks," I say, "I would like to call for twenty volunteers to come up here and participate." People start making a line.

"As you can see, I have set up an easel with a sheet of white paper. And here in my hand is an ink pad. I would like to ask each of you to press your thumb firmly into the ink and then leave your print on the paper. Good. Now one more thing. Here's a pen, and please, each of you, write your last name very clearly beneath your thumbprint. Here's a box of tissues for you to wipe the ink off with."

I am terrified. Rehearsals back at the hotel room went...poorly, and right now she is paying full attention only to her knee, where she's managed to draw blood. Some has gotten on the hem of her dress.

A woman writes her name beneath her thumbprint and then offers Pam a tissue—no reaction—which finally just floats to the floor, landing on the sketchpad.

Once the easel sheet has accumulated its twenty nice sharp thumbprints, two rows of ten, each captioned with a name, I thank the volunteers. The last two are returning to their seats.

"At this time, I am going to show your prints to my daughter for a period of *five seconds*. As you have noticed, she has been somewhat...preoccupied and has not yet even peeked at your contributions yet."

I lift the easel and place it down right beside the bloody knee. "Pam, darling, *here are the prints*." Nothing. An uncomfortable hush descends over the audience. Our career is free-falling right through this stage floor.

I am just about to pull the plug and go to an old, boring card trick when she glances up—and I mean *glances*—at the easel. I absolutely cannot believe that that was long enough, even for her, but I decide to plow ahead. She's put me in an impossible position.

"Okay, that's apparently all the time she needs, ladies and gentlemen!"

Pam switches knees and starts in on the second scab. I fight back my gag reflex. "I would like to ask one of you to come forward again. You, sir? Yes, that's terrific. Please return to the stage, if you would. I know, I'm giving you quite a workout ha ha."

While he makes his way up here, I rip off the page with 211 written on it, place the sketchpad back on her lap, then jam the marker into her hand.

"That's great, sir, now would you please show the girl your thumb." He laughs but does what he's told. He's partially wiped the ink off his skin but you can still clearly make out the pattern—actually, even *more* clearly in the residue. I counted on this side effect, having tested on myself.

Again, Pam glances. Then her marker squeaks on the pad. I feel like a member of the audience myself, all in the dark.

"Sir, may I ask your name?"

He clears his throat and speaks directly into the microphone. "I'm Roger Rosenberg."

I check the pad first myself to make sure, then pick it up and hold it high for everyone to bathe in.

ROSENBERG

Standing ovation! The conference chairman runs back on stage.

When the wild applause finally subsides, he says, "That was perhaps the most remarkable demonstration of eidetic memory I have ever witnessed. Can you share us how you did that, Sweetheart? I mean, what did it feel like from *your* point of view?"

He leans down and holds the mic up to Pam's mouth. Good

luck with that. Some autism expert. But she does speak. "So...frogs cannot vomit. If they try to vomit, their whole stomach comes out."

Roaring laughter. I want to hug her. The chairman goes, "Look, Sweetheart, look how *happy* you've made everybody. Do you realize it? I wonder what you see when you look out there at your admirers."

I'm starving. No more milk for me. Great White stole my milk forever. I don't even want to go back in the goat-house. And now I can't trust any food in the house, either.

On my Kindle, I'm learning what is safe to eat in the woods, then looking up plants on Google Images. Leaning against the Single Thing. Chewing clover, burdock, dandelions. Clover and burdock leaves taste okay. Dandelions do not.

So...there are many choices of tree bark that can be eaten. In fact, the Native Americans used certain tree barks as dietary supplements. Some of the most popular edible choices are aspen, birch, willow, maple, and pine trees.

Light red ants taste sweet. Beetles taste like crunchy soap.

The most interesting part about including edible insects in your daily diet in a time of emergency or food shortage is this: bugs provide protein. When eaten together with specific types of wild plants, they can meet all our nutritional requirements for healthy living.

I'm on the ridge. Leaning against the Single Thing. The whole forest gathers me back together. Well, it used to. It still does. But now I feel like there are eyes watching me from every direction. Maybe. Who made the t-pee and piled up those rocks?

Some person? Must be.

I'm suddenly afraid to go back to the t-pee. Like I'm on stage again. But I won't do any tricks. I won't do tricks any more forever.

With my own eyes, I am taking hundreds of pictures. Checking for changes from second to second. This is not a trick. This is what my eyes are *for*. clickclickclickclick. I divide the space of the world into squares. Just like in Minecraft. Here in the woods, every square holds its own complicated pattern of tree trunks and branches and leaves and shadows. Every square holds a completely different pattern. Fingerprints are a lot easier because they are all the same. Almost the same. The little differences pop out.

click. click. click. click.

Luckily, there is no wind in this world today. I love my wind but not for taking pictures. I need complete stillness so I can compare the same square again and again for changes. So I can see who is here with me. It has to be a person. Or something else with hands.

Maybe I am taking thousands of pictures, not hundreds. I'm not counting. I'm holding my head perfectly still. So…animals in the wild will scan their surroundings for hours. I often pretend to be a predator. Predators must know the precise distance of their prey to attack them with assurance of success. Many visual cues are available so that no movements of the head or body are required. That would alert prey. Many species have telephoto optics, which magnify the retinal image.

clickclickclickclickclickclick

But today I am not a predator. I think I might be prey. I have never been prey before, so I don't know how. I am trying to learn a new way of seeing. So…prey animals usually have eyes set on the sides of their head. This gives them better peripheral vision and enables them to detect danger within a wider field of vision.

Trying to use my left eye for over there, my right eye for over there. Both at the same time. click. click. Ouch. I've never used my eyes like two different cameras before.

I close them for a rest and press them with my thumbs. After twenty-two seconds, the yellow bursts of light come up. I can also make spinning wheels of friendly flame by pressing my eyes like this.

When I open them and blink, the world has turned pale around me. With floating see-through patches, like it's shedding its thin skin.

I'm starving. It's time to be a predator again. I will need to learn to catch real animals for meat. Soon. Right now, I'll stay alive on what I can find. Because this is a time of emergency and food shortage.

Okay, Jimmy Fallon it ain't, but hey, it's still TV—a show out of Ohio, "Good Morning Cincinnati!"

Several people in Kansas City videotaped and posted the thumbprint trick and oh man! Can you spell V-I-R-A-L?

How did I even think of that trick in the first place? It was one day when she was little, back before she hated me. She would hold my left hand—always the *left*—and stare at it for hours, the lines on the palm, my knuckles, bending everything to make creases. All five fingerprints, over and over, checking and rechecking. Each time, she'd notice that the thumbprint pattern didn't match the other four...and this totally cracked her up.

This one day, I found a notebook in her room. It was chock full of drawings of my thumbprints! I'm talking *exact replicas*, from memory. I got an ink pad later to confirm it.

The girl was four years old.

Through the wall, Great White's snoring is deep and regular every four seconds. The rhythm calms me down.

I had to wait till his light went off before I snuck into the house. It was raining and I haven't built a shelter on the ridge yet. After the sleeping poison, no more goat-house. And I'm scared to go back to the t-pee.

My stomach hurts. My eyes ache from taking pictures all day. And from pressing them. The person is sure good at hiding.

I am finally warm and dry in bed. Even wild animals sometimes prefer a soft place to lie down. Their dens are often lined with grass, soil, and even feathers.

The goat-house floor made me forget how much I used to love this bed. My wind rattles the window glass. Each pane gets its own attention tonight.

My head fills with a super-fast slide show. At first, it's the little squares of woods again, all the patterns making me laugh and laugh. They are so different! And then, every once in a while, a long-ago picture takes the place of a forest square, like someone is sticking it in there by mistake.

I see my old cat Benjamin. Good cat. I see pictures of him in all kinds of light and all kinds of sleeping positions. She took him away when she left.

I see her index finger with a short row of dots across it. This means she let me bite her finger and didn't get mad, because I was gentle. My teeth must have been very small, from those dots.

I see her and Great White laughing together in the yard. They are leaning against the car. Laughing at something I'm doing.

Probably spinning and flipping on the grass. I remember trying to make them laugh when she still lived here with us.

tink...tink...tink

I sit up in bed. I have been asleep. Outside, my wind has stopped dead.

tink...tink.

Sounds like pebbles hitting the metal roof over my window. Pebbles from the wall of roots. They hit and then roll down, hit then roll down, bouncing. *tink_{tinktink}*.

I see one fall past the windowpanes. I see it in the dim moonlight. Somebody is tossing them onto the *roof*. My clock says 3:24. Someone is *tossing* them.

I listen to make sure Great White is still in his room. His snores are softer now but there they are.

I listen but nothing. It's the person from the woods. It has to be. We live on a dead-end road and our nearest neighbor is six point nine miles away.

Only a hand with fingers can toss pebbles. Well, or maybe a bird could drop them from its beak but not in the same spot every time unless it is sitting on a branch. There was a tree it could have used. But that tree fell down.

I stare out the window and rock back and forth on my bed. I flap my hands and slap my head. I do all this quietly.

3:29.

3:42.

A loud slap on the side of the goat-house.

The goats go *MEHHHHHH! MEHHHHHH! MEHHHHHH!* And then BANG!

A rock just hit the roof over my room. Where did it go? Where did it come from?

Great White's door opens and then mine opens.

"What the hell are you doing in here?" I go into my ball. Out the corner of my eye I see his hair all messed up. "You hit my wall just to wake me up! Holy crap! Why would you do a thing like that? I've got a ton of work to do tomorrow...for *us*."

He slams my door and then slams his door.

I stare at the wild animal posters on my wall. In the moonlight. Cheetah running. Elephant trumpeting. Peregrine falcon diving from the sky.

I go and kneel at the window, hurting my scabs. Sway back and forth, back and forth, back and forth. Taking pictures of the goat-house. Pictures of the fallen tree. Wall of roots. Pictures of the blue pool and the apple tree.

Then I get braver...forest forest forest forest forest forest....

4:04.

Bright moonlight pictures. I keep looking for creepers and zombies and skeletons. No. Stop. This is real life, not Minecraft.

4:34.

Should I be more afraid? 4:58.

She's not in her room. Lucky for her. Little brat was trying to sabotage me last night.

Kneeling beside her kiddie pool, I splash as loudly as I can. Sometimes this will draw her in. Probably doesn't even remember the city pool or how we always used to play together, back in the day, but she loves to splash here.

Up in the woods, I hear her knocking something against a tree. That's another first. Probably calling for food, which is a good sign.

Back at my desk, I utilize what I've been learning from the Social Media Marketing podcasts. Networking and outreach.

I have created a Facebook page called "Kid Genius! Pamela Manchester: Public Figure" and feature the Kansas City video, which already has 44,132 views on YouTube! Make that 44,213.

I could sit here "refreshing" all day long.

"Good Morning Cincinnati!" is nailed down for next week, and now a handful of new offers have come in overnight.

Through my open window, I hear two more knocks in the woods. I will offer her some almond butter toast on the fallen tree. Start building up trust again. High-maintenance child or what? I need to keep her healthy and I guess she's thinking twice now about goat's milk. She does like toast. She's not allergic to almond butter or gluten-free bread.

Hey, a Facebook message popping up...

> Dear Mr. Manchester, we are extremely impressed by your daughter's remarkable abilities and would like to invite her to demonstrate them at our Third Annual International Celebration of the Brain, which takes place this fall, October 4-8. I'm linking all the necessary information for you. We offer compensation of $5000, as well as travel expenses and room/board during your stay in beautiful San Francisco. Here at the Institute, we are working to push back the boundaries of human knowledge of the brain and its true bla bla, so that one day bla bla blabidy bla...

Book it!

It's a dead rabbit. When I got here this morning, the body was laid neatly on top of the Single Thing like a fur hat. Too small for this head. No blood but its back legs are all broken and twisted. At first, I started running in circles, frightened that the person would kill me next and twist my legs.

But then, I remembered when I was up here yesterday. How I

thought about hunting animals for meat. I was thinking that and now this rabbit. I sat down on the ground and started rocking back and forth, flapping my hands and slapping my head to get all the new energy out. So hilarious!

I'm still laughing when I hear the knocks. Sounds like the person is smacking a tree, one, two, three times. Hard. Strong. Somewhere farther up the ridge.

Now I'm back afraid. Not all the way back, not running in circles. I stand up and take pictures. I wonder what the person is trying to say to me.

I know it's a person, not an animal or a ghost, but the scary thing is I don't know what it looks like. I know it is nice because of the rabbit. I know it is powerful because of the rock on my roof last night. But I have no idea what kind of size or shape or even skin to give the person, in my mind.

knock...knock...................KNOCK! A little closer this time.

I swallow.

knock...knock...................KNOCK!

eat...that............ BUNNY!

I swallow again, this time with pretend rabbit blood in my throat. *Gag!*

I pick up the brown floppy body and sling it over my shoulder. Heading down the hill toward the kitchen. I have cooked in the kitchen before. I stop halfway. Angry at myself.

What kind of wild animal gags on its own prey? And goes to cook in a kitchen?

I march back up the hill. Lean against the Single Thing. Toss the rabbit on the ground in front of me. I stare at its little face.

So...when tearing apart flesh and muscle, a predator will often ingest the chunks without even chewing. At other times, it will only drink the blood, which provides nourishment and hydration if water is scarce.

FATAL

Three days later, everything has changed.

"Mr. Manchester," says Doctor Halloway.

"Jim's fine."

"She should really be admitted to the hospital and will need to be if you can't keep her in bed and stick to the antibiotic schedule."

I'll have to pay extra for this house call, but when I tried to carry her to the car she almost bit me. No sense both of us catching this disease, whatever it is. And this is still way cheaper than an ambulance.

She won't swallow the pills so the doctor injects her in the butt. You'd think she was being murdered!

Speaking of which, I can't get the image out of my mind. She showed up in the back yard looking like the victim of a knife attack. At first, I naturally thought it was *her* blood, so I chased her, hoping to pin her down and locate the wounds. She wouldn't let me get close, and we ran around the yard, the whole thing looking like some wacky scene from a movie.

Eventually, we both got tired and sat down, a healthy distance apart, and then I could see she wasn't bleeding anywhere. The red was thick around her mouth, thinning out across her face and neck. Some in her hair, too. In other words, she must have killed and eaten some raw animal—*Here we go, here's the next stage of her revenge against me, just because I laced that damn nanny goat's teat and gave her a free trip to Kansas City and true stardom.*

I decided not to give her any more satisfaction, so I returned to the house and my computer screen—my little window to the reasonable outside world.

That would have been the end of it—let her wash up or not

wash up—if yesterday Pam hadn't started trembling and throwing up.

She finally came inside and crawled in bed. I found her old potty in the basement and dropped it in the corner of her room. Later, I collected a stool sample in a jar and delivered it to the hospital myself. This morning I get a call with the results—tularemia.

"Because of her autism and combative tendencies," the doc continues, "caring for her here will be difficult. I've given her the first mega-dose and I've written out these instructions. You can dissolve the pills in orange juice or water. This tularemia bacterium is highly.... Jim, it's dangerous. It may easily develop into sepsis, which if untreated can be...fatal."

To make sure Pam didn't hear that last word, I glance down and find her still very much asleep on top of her covers—rapid breathing, covered in sweat, face white as chalk. When she's clean and indoors, the girl is beautiful. Thank God I washed the blood away, peeled off her filthy clothes, and wrestled her into pajamas before Doctor Doom showed up. Wouldn't want him to think I'm raising some painted savage.

He's a gray old man with a bad limp and small, disappointed eyes. He looks at me like I'm risking my own child's life. I'm tempted to sit him down and show him the video of the thumbprint trick and all the love from that audience, pouring over her.

"What has she been eating?"

"Oh...well, the poor girl's allergic to most foods, so we keep it simple. Goat's milk. Toast. Almond butter. Fresh fruits and vegetables, of course. Plenty of those."

Doctor Halloway actually scratches his head. "The tularemia bacterium has an incubation period, typically, of two to five days. Is there any chance she has handled raw or undercooked meat when she was out of your sight?"

"That is...no, that's not likely. I keep a pretty strict eye—hey, but she *does* spend time with the goats out there. They could carry this bug, right? I'll bet that's it."

"Well, she would have to handle or consume their *meat*, Jim." He starts gently checking her body. "Or maybe if they'd...bitten her and broken the skin somewhere. What's this in her hair. Is it blood?"

"This? No, that's dried paint. She loves to paint but she's sloppy. I combed most of it out."

"As far as I can tell, she has no injuries other than those two skinned knees. Tularemia is usually transferred from game animals. Hunters will catch it by dressing out their kills with an open cut on their hand. It's also known as 'rabbit fever.'"

"Huh. Strange case, I guess."

The person didn't mean it. He didn't mean to hurt me. I got sick because I'm not wild enough. Not yet.

I kneel at my window all day. Use a pillow for my sore knees. Swaying and swaying. Scanning the forest for any changes. I stare at the fallen tree. Maybe a head will pop up there.

I have eighty-nine Minecraft worlds waiting for me, but I'm here at the window instead. The person is still hiding in the woods. Probably, the animals have seen him. I stare at them when they pass by. Deer. Crows. Squirrels. Maybe I can see through their eyes.

I tell the Single Thing to keep a look-out, too. I'll be back up there soon.

I still don't know what to picture, but I can hear the person knocking on trees again, far away. The window only opens five inches, but I can smell the exact trees it's knocking on.

Great White never knocks on my door, but his footsteps in the hall warn me to jump back into bed every time. Before he comes in.

He gives me Diet Cokes. I drink them because I am very thirsty. I don't think there is sleeping poison in them. He wouldn't want to make me any sicker.

I am feeling much stronger. I keep pretending. I threw up in the potty on purpose. He can't drag me onto another airplane if I'm still sick. F-A-T-A-L.

I keep her room locked, of course, to protect her from herself. Her window frame is warped so the window hardly opens. Can't afford to lose her to damn nature again. So far, she hasn't tried to hide by the door and charge through when I open it. She hasn't hurled objects at my head. I'm ready for anything, but every time I check she's just lying in bed, staring into space, still trembling, panting, too weak to even play on her Kindle.

I must say, I am taking excellent care of her—doses of Cipro right on time, dissolved in Diet Coke, which she can't resist. These past four days, I feel like I have a baby girl again, feeding her bottles. *Eat your heart out, Helen.* I think this might be a turning point for us, a brand new start.

Little does she know that right down the hall in my office, her career is exploding. It killed me to have to cancel "Good Morning Cincinnati!" But right away, replacements cropped up and now we're on a major road trip next month. She'll be tip-top again by then.

Every sunset, I lie here listening for pebbles on the roof. I finally decide to close the window. It was closed when the pebbles came last time. My wind rattles the panes, feeling left out.

I sleep sometimes.

3:55 AM, Great White starts snoring through the wall. That's good, that's the same as before, too.

4:39, I hear something outside. I sit up in bed. Same.

It's not pebbles on the roof or a rock. No banging the goat-house wall. I can hear their hooves nervous on the floor. My wind has gone dead quiet again. Everybody is listening.

tap tap tap taptaptap Somewhere in the woods.

I go to the windowsill.

tap tap tap tap taptap

I tap the glass with my fingernail.

The person taps back.

This is really happening.

Or is it just a woodpecker?

I open the window its five inches and aim my ear through.

tap tap tap taptaptap Much closer now.

A tiny amount of dawn is lifting the ground. I scan with my eyes and click square pictures all across the edge, till two of the same spot don't match from one to the next. I focus there. Behind the goat-house. clickclickclickclick.

A shadow shape sways back and forth between two trees. Back and forth. Under thick leaves where dawn is slower.

I blink and blink. I can't see the shape of the shape but it's not a woodpecker. It copies me. I sway some more and more. We both do.

"Person?" I whisper through the five inches.

I stand and muscle the window open another inch or two. Stick my whole head out.

I whisper, "Person?"

"Hey, Little Ticket, guess what?" I throw open her door. "We've got baby goats!"

Nobody home.

When the sun needles my eyes, it always makes me laugh so much. This morning, I don't have time for our game. I'm busy breaking branches, oak and pine. I've got my sleeves rolled up and I have a whole pile next to me. I'm out of breath because these branches are thick. I have to rest every few minutes. Still some rabbit fever.

My shelter will be better than the t-pee. I don't know what shape to choose yet. And the person will be allowed to come inside anytime he wants to. I'll make it big enough for us both.

I'm not afraid of him anymore because he was swaying so gently by the goat-house.

Also, the rabbit. I think that was a test. I ate it. I passed the test. I didn't die.

When I wiggled through the window and landed on the ground, I looked between those two trees. The swaying shadow was gone. I knocked with my tongue on the roof of my mouth *tock tock tock tock*

All I wanted to do was run after the person. It was still pretty dark and chilly out here. My wind patted me on the face, telling me wait a little. Wait a little. My thin blue pajamas rippled.

When the sun came up, I used the old path. Bare feet. No tripping.

Now I grab and twist one last branch...*CRACK!*...and I'm done. The Single Thing has been watching the whole time, proud of me. All this work. Time to lie down beside the pile and rest. I've never been up here in pajamas before.

I let the sun sink into my bones and light them up. I close my eyes and watch the pale red of my eyelids. Just the same color as my ants. I picture them carrying their eggs away from danger. Then, I watch my skeleton breathing. I can look at myself from the outside sometimes. I can look at any part of my skeleton. I search the foot bones first. click click click. I zoom in there for close-up pictures. My feet are cold but the more I zoom in the more the sun fills each tiny bone. So...there are twenty-six bones in the human foot. One quarter of all the bones in the body.

When the bones in my foot are full of sun they start to glow. I switch to the other foot.

mehhhhhh! mehhhhhh!

I sit up. I'd know that sound anywhere. We've had babies before.

mehhhhhh!

It is coming up the hill. I smile for it.

Wait a minute. How can a goat be coming up the hill if it was just born?

I bolt. My feet do not make any noise.

"Pam!"

Great White can't see me hiding behind this thick bush. He's got the baby under his arm and a bottle of Diet Coke in his hand. "Where are you? I've got a brand new friend for you. You can *name* him."

He has no idea how close he is. My wind blows a swirl around all three of us.

"Pam!"

I lift a flat rock and find another ant colony. Again, they carry pale eggs in their jaws. So hilarious! One second you are just living in your world, doing all your little jobs. You never saw sunlight before on your colony. Ever. But you know exactly what to do. Hide them! Hide our eggs! The role of reproduction is to provide for the continued existence of a species. It is the process by which living organisms duplicate themselves.

The nanny goat did it, too. Everybody is doing it.

The baby in Great White's arms struggles to get free. I can't make a noise or he will see me. Now he's walking in the wrong direction! Stop!

"Listen, Pam, you need to take your medicine and get back to bed. You are still a very sick child, Honey. I'm sure you don't want to have to go to the hosp—"

He stops. I can't watch.

"Holy

crap!"

It's her. Helen. Her *head*. At first, I think it's her *actual* head until I get my bearings and realize how big it is. Pam must have *sculpted* it. Amazing.

But what sends me tripping over backward, landing on my ass—Diet Coke and goat flying through the air—is that look on her face. It's the same smug expression she'd always get when she thought I'd screwed up in some way.

The baby runs in circles, its legs buckling.

"Pam! I know you're here!! You've got a lot of explaining to do!"

Breathe, Jim.

"Okay, all right. I don't know what to say about your...impressive art project here, but I'm going to let it slide for the moment."

I stand up and brush off my pants. "Nearly gave me a stroke." I make one half-hearted swipe at the goat. "I'm just going to go back down and figure out what to do with you. For now, there's the soda on the ground. Drink it. It's got your medicine in it and *I am trusting you*. I will bring you another one tonight. Do *not* kill and eat any more animals. If you want food, come down and I will be happy to fix you something. Or hey, knock on a tree like before and I'll bring your lunch up here."

A good father, within the confines I'm given.

When he's definitely gone, my wind shivers the bush to let me know. I cross the meadow. From out of sight, the baby says *mehhhhhh!*

"You're lost."

I tried not to listen to Great White. But it's true. I'm hungry. I need to find some more grasshoppers. They were the best bugs so far. Kind of like pistachios.

I spot the Coke bottle on some moss and pick it up.

I go sit against the Single Thing. Leaning back. "Sorry he saw you."

I am in a bad mood. I jab my left elbow into my hip bone. To make my funny bone go *twang*. When the feeling wears off, I do it again. And again. It always makes me laugh. So...in human anatomy, the ulnar nerve is the largest unprotected nerve in the body. The name "funny bone" is thought to refer to the peculiar sensation experienced when it is struck.

The baby comes bouncing out of some ferns and heads

straight toward me. Then, it gets scared and spins away. Then, it stands looking at me.

mehhhhhh! mehhhhhh! mehhhhhh!

I know I am *supposed* to love it, but I do. I click pictures of its fuzzy legs, and especially the knees, which look way too big. The size of ping pong balls.

"How can I be wild?" I ask the baby. "How can I be wild? How can *we* be wild?"

The baby licks its lips.

I go back to scanning my environment, like a predator. What you have to do is tear off the grasshoppers' legs and wings. "You really don't want those," I say.

The baby needs somebody to teach her. She is sniffing the air. I think she's a girl. I'm going to call her Knees. Knees the Newest Girl on the Planet. I feel like I'm a new girl, too. Now that I live on the ridge. We live on the ridge.

I snap my fingers for her. She bolts back into the ferns. She just wants her Mama. I miss that milk, too.

When I unscrew the Diet Coke bottle, a tall spray launches out. Before I can shriek somebody else does. Sounds like a trumpeting elephant with its trunk held high. It's a person with its head tucked low.

I am used to seeing people.

And then, I remember. *The person.*

Hunched down behind a tree on the other side of the meadow. I can see half the face peeking out.

When I laugh, the one eye blinks.

I take plenty of close-ups till I can tell it's a boy, not a girl, even though he's got long brown hair down to his shoulder. Under that hair, his shoulder has hair too, the color of chestnut. I guess when you are a wild person, your get to have hair on your shoulders.

I look down at the smooth white skin of my own arms and shoulders. When I check back, the boy is gone.

clickclickclickclickclickclickclickclickclickclickclickclick
clickclickclickclickclickclickclickclickclickclickclickclick

There he is. Running away down a trail.

It's a fresh trail. I never noticed it before.

I can only see him for a few clicks. Hs hairy back and legs. You get hair there, too.

The trail goes down the far side of the ridge into a valley. I have never been there. It is a dark valley. Dark even in daytime.

I drink what's left in the bottle. Just some foam.

I've never been down into that valley because what I like to do is the same thing every, every day. Before the tree fell, I always walked up the old path, 1498 steps. Spent my days working on the Single Thing. Leaning against it. Talking to it, feeling solid. And paying attention to the details of the world. There was plenty up here to learn about.

But now, everything is different. There is a wild boy. I live up here full time now. I need to explore my environment. Find out how to survive. I'm going to learn to be wild and never let Great White control me again, or even *see* me. I've been preparing for this my whole life.

I stand and follow the new trail. Very, very slowly. This trail is not like others. Ferns in the middle are all flattened down. Tree branches on both sides are snapped off.

Farther along, I notice more t-pees. Way too small to crawl inside of. Made out of branches with all the bark peeled off. Naked little branches. My skeleton bones.

Up ahead, a young birch bends over the trail. A perfect archway. The top is above my head. On the other side, the trail starts down steeply. I take ten pictures per second to make sure it's safe.

Behind me, from a great distance, *meeeeeeeeeeh!*

When I step through this doorway, nothing happens. And then, nothing happens some more. I try breathing, but that's a mistake. I'm knocked backward by two explosions down in the valley.

Back at the Single Thing, I hug it. Crying.

"Calm down, calm down," it tells me. "Those were not explosions but just a tree. The first sound was the tree trunk breaking. The second sound was the tree hitting to the ground."

I lean back against the pebbly lips and chin. Breathing in and breathing out.

"That's one powerful boy."

Doctor Halloway must have spoken to her.

Marlene Stevens, our old therapist, pulls into our driveway, wearing a very smug expression of her own.

She climbs out and shuts her door, just standing there waiting. Looking around, already taking mental notes.

I do *not* have time for this.

I'm awake, I'm awake. I was in Minecraft. A Creeper blew himself up right beside me.

From somewhere, a rock sails through the air and lands two feet from me and the Single Thing. Bounces away.

I need to find water to drink and drink. And wash my wrist. It has sticky, annoying Diet Cole on it. And I have to pee. All three.

But I don't dare move a muscle.

After a minute, another rock strikes the dirt. I still can't figure out where it came from. When it rolls to a stop, it looks like the ones from inside that first t-pee.

Waiting for another rock, I go to the edge of the meadow. My bathroom spot. I always bury number twos but pee on the brown ferns. As I finish, I'm lucky to be looking in the right direction. The next rock comes up from darkness into sunlight. Bending through the sky. Smacking the dirt beside me.

"How did you know where to aim?" This is the first time I have spoken to a person, besides facts about science. I didn't mean to. It was a mistake. I want to explode like a Creeper into dust.

I pull up my pants. Go into my ball. Rock back and forth, faster and faster.

tap tap tap tap

I don't know if I've been rocking for two minutes or two hours. The taps are so quiet I might not have really heard them. My hair is all stuck to my face. Old crying. I sit up and scan around. clickclick? No more taps to help me.

When I spot the boy it is only by luck. He is on a limb inside a tree. My wind moved his leaves aside for a moment so I could see him squatting. Like me peeing. Around his eyes he has skin without hair. The color of birch bark. His thick knees are pointing toward me. One hand holds a branch up by his head.

When the leaves settle back in place, all I can see is one eye again. Black. Blink. And some of the longer hair down the side of his head.

"Can you..." I cough, acid rising in my throat. Talking to a person is the hardest thing to do on Earth. I have never wanted to do it before today. "Can you teach me to be wild?"

The eye blinks again. My wind tosses the boy's hair and my hair at the same time.

clickclickclickclick

Suddenly, between one click and the next, he disappears. I hear him thud onto hard ground. His footsteps fade quickly into the valley.

A minute later, I hear voices down below. Great White and a woman. Getting closer.

I run to the boy's same tree and hide behind it.

"I'll admit you're right, Mr. Manchester, this is a remarkable sculpture that Pamela has made out of natural materials. The resemblance is...well, as far as I can remember, it's Helen."

I recognize this woman from long in the past. From an office. I liked her because she stood up to Great White.

"But you understand, Mr. Manchester, she simply cannot be permitted to—"

"I'm sure she's watching us right now, Marlene. She never goes too far. And I have a plan to capt—to bring her home this afternoon."

He's got another bottle of Diet Coke in his hand. That one won't fool me. That one I'll be pouring out on the ground. No matter how thirsty I am.

He sets it carefully on top of the Single Thing. Where the rabbit was.

"Pamela, Honey, are you here? Your father and I are very concerned about you." She slaps a mosquito on her arm, then another on her ear. "Please at least make some sound to show us that you're here."

If Knees went *meh!* right now, I would have to laugh.

"Given her medical condition..." The woman faces him with her hands on her hips. "...this situation is extremely serious. I would hate for it to escalate...on my end. You know...in terms of the State."

"Ha ha, yes!" Great White slaps her on the shoulder. She steps away. "Yes, I'm aware. You don't have to draw me a picture."

The woman is already heading back down the old path. Great White is whining behind her. "She'll be in her room again by bedtime, right on schedule with her meds, I promise. Mar—Doctor Stevens? Please give me that chance before you make any calls."

They don't belong here.

"*Bitch*. Making me *beg*. Come to *my* house threatening to call the authorities. I could have shown her the Kansas City video...why give her the satisfaction?"

She's got me babbling to myself like one of her wingnuts at the clinic. But *unlike* a wingnut at the clinic—*hello!*—I am a highly effective person.

For example, I've got rope and two hours of daylight left. Binoculars hanging around my neck and a compass in my pocket. Haul her back here long before dark. Shouldn't need the rope if she drank that last Diet Coke.

On my way past the goat-house and into the woods, the nanny is still calling for her lost kid. *Know how you feel, old girl...*

Two steps in, I remember the rocks—target practice. This time she might not miss me on purpose. I climb the hill with my arm raised, guarding my skull.

Yup, empty bottle sitting on top of Helen. I bonk her with it on the forehead. "Bet you wish you'd thought of this, dear. Would have made your life a lot easier."

Now to locate Sleeping Beauty...

Probably, she had time to pick a soft place to land, so I circle the clearing until I almost trip over Pam's latest conquest. I can hardly believe it's come to this, but obviously. *Holy crap*—the goat's whole back half is gone. Not even bones around. I hold my nose. It doesn't look rotten yet but it sure smells. I won't be sending a picture of this to Social Services any time soon, even though, c'mon, she's protected—it's not like I forgot to add her medicine to the sleepy-time Diet Coke, too. Actually, it's like *two* kinds of medicine. I mean, doesn't a sick child need plenty of shut-eye?

She can't have gotten far. As I walk, I listen for her breathing. Instead, there is a thump-thump-thump in the woods on the far side of the ridge. Like somebody's pounding the turf down below. And then, it switches to a kind of popping sound, like you'd make with your lips. I freeze in place.

"Pam...?" Of all the hundred really bizarre sounds she makes, I've never heard these before. "That you?"

Footsteps from the same direction. I stop and they stop. I start again and...*Crap*. Much heavier than my daughter could make, and right in the middle of my chest, I feel a low vibration. It reminds me of standing too close to a speaker at a concert, but that never came with this fear.

I can't move my legs. I can't move my legs. I'm just standing here like a statue and right away, for some reason, I know exactly where to look.

I am not seeing that.

At the edge of the clearing, half in shade, there stands a man. Only it is not a man. Instead of clothes or skin, it has reddish-brown hair. And it is much, much, much larger than I am. Twice as tall. Its head is shaped like a gorilla's head but its eyes, nose, and mouth are human. *Look* human.

Please please please let me move.

It is swaying back and forth like some hideous parody of my daughter. Glaring directly at my chest, locking me down as if its hand is squeezing my heart. I cannot quite breathe.

"So...giraffes and humans have the same number of bones in their necks: seven."

Pam's voice breaks the spell and I can suddenly bend my elbows. Then my knees. Sounds like she's floating somewhere above my shoulder.

But I'm already running like holy hell back down the hill. I keep getting smacked in the face by branches, and then I trip on a root and feel myself launching through space.

I lay poor Knees out gently on a bed of moss, what's left of her. I do understand that a wild girl would never cry at a thing like this.

Her blood is all over my blue pajamas because I've been carrying her up from the valley. Her back half is gone. I don't look at her face. Or the lips that she was licking. What I look at are her two front hooves, which are glossy, black, and new.

I found her in the valley. I went down there because I had to. I needed to wash my wrist and dunk my head in cold, running water. And drink. I knew that streams are frequently found in valleys. I didn't have time to be afraid anymore. My skin was hot again and I'd never been so thirsty in my whole life. A thirst that clutched at my throat from the inside. And I knew the wild boy would not hurt me.

Beside the stream. That's where I found Knees. Smashed on a rock and chewed. I threw up and had to drink more water.

I carried her back up.

I'm just about to dig a hole for her. I hear Great White knocking on the Single Thing with the empty bottle *thock thock*, saying mean words. This makes me sicker.

He should easily spot me, except he's too blind and dumb. I sneak away into the shadows to the wild boy's climbing tree. I feel weak. I hardly make it up to the sitting limb.

Look at that rope looped around his arm. Great White is

hunting for my floppy body. All poisoned to tie up. He thinks I drank that Diet Coke instead of pouring it onto the dirt.

My fever-forehead sends purple beams of hate toward him and he goes completely stiff, staring into the woods.

I'm blocked by leaves, but the look on his face tells me he has seen the wild boy.

I look again at Great White's rope and start to panic. I tell myself to calm down because he can't possibly catch the wild boy. It looks like he can't even move. I can't help it. I can't think what to do or what to say. I have to make something happen.

"So...giraffes and humans have the same number of bones in their necks: seven."

Great White suddenly turns and runs beneath my branch. He doesn't use the old path and soon stumbles full speed into a tree. While he's still in the air, I click many pictures, trying to slow him down. His head hits the trunk anyway. Then, clickclick clickclickclickclickclickclickclickclickclick as he rolls and rolls to a stop.

I jump down and no, it's not the wild boy that he saw. It's some kind of giant muscle man as tall as my bedroom ceiling. His hair is redder than the wild boy's. I'd be terrified if this was real but it is only a cartoon dream. I don't even have to take any pictures. Except one little bubble in my head thinks differently. It thinks, There is a *family* of them out here!

He looks me up and down once, then turns to go. I sniff sniff sniff sniff. Like rotten eggs mixed with my old cat Benjamin's litter box when it needed changing. He doesn't bob up and down at all when he walks. He's perfectly smooth, like he's riding a rail back into the valley. Taking his stink with him.

My wind ruffles Great White's hair. His nose is bleeding. I crawl closer down the bank and finally see the chest rising and falling. As long as he's not awake, I can sit here beside him, pretend he's a big ragdoll. "So...woodpeckers slam their heads into wood at a rate of twenty pecks per second. They are protected from injury by a spongy area that sits behind their beaks and acts as a shock absorber."

Far away, I hear a deep voice, like a father punishing a child. Is the wild boy in trouble?

"So...the brain of a cockroach is located inside its body," I explain to the floppy doll. "If a cockroach loses its head, it can live up to nine days. A decapitated cockroach dies only because it cannot *eat*."

The eyes flutter.

That was a fucking Bigfoot.

I'm at the desk with an ice pack on my nose. I probably have a concussion, but I'm sorry, this is too important. Google quickly leads me to the Bigfoot Field Researchers Organization and its national database of reports, including some right nearby.

> YEAR: 2000
> SEASON: Spring
> MONTH: May
> STATE: Minnesota
> COUNTY: St. Louis
> NEAREST TOWN: Virginia

That's like half an hour west of here!

> OBSERVED: I was riding a bicycle north of Virginia on a small dirt road. I saw a creature about 300 feet to the northwest of me on a hill at the edge of a mixed deciduous and evergreen forest. It looked at me, turned, crouched, and walked up the hill into the forest. It looked cautious and apprehensive. It had black fur and a very hairy face more like a man than a bear (it had

no snout). It walked upright like a man. It did not move or look like a bear. My impression was that it had sense of humanness about it, but it was a wild, unkempt, hairy creature. I was quite scared and turned and got out of there in the opposite direction.

YEAR: 2012
SEASON: Fall
MONTH: September
DATE: Labor Day
STATE: Minnesota
COUNTY: St. Louis
NEAREST TOWN: Skibo

Twenty minutes south!

OBSERVED: Large figure walking through the tree line. About 7-7.5 feet tall. I was about 20-22 yards away. It was a reddish brown color. I saw from mid-shoulder to top of its head. The color was a reddish brown but a bit darker on the head. The hair was also shorter on the head than the shoulders, wiry hair, kinda scraggy. Flatter face the head was really long almost like it was a cone or a peak at the top. I was frozen when I saw this creature I couldn't move for like 4 seconds, after that 4 seconds I turned to my friend to see if he also saw it, when I looked back the creature was gone. There was also a very musky smell during this time.

"Musky," I'll say.

I research long into the night, fanning out all across Minnesota, ignoring the nonstop pings from Pam's "Kid Genius!" Facebook page. I've never before paid attention to this stupid topic—*Bigfoot, yeah right*—but now it's not just a *topic* anymore, is it?

I still can't believe it. And I can't believe he was swaying back and forth, as if he needed to be *more intimidating* than just looming over me, a thousand pounds of pure muscle.

If I can get video footage of what I saw up there today—which shouldn't be difficult, if he'll just provide a repeat performance—I won't need to peddle Pam's tricks anymore. That world will pale in comparison.

I remember that famous old movie, the Patterson Film, that supposedly shows one of these ape creatures walking and swinging its arms. Even though most people think it's a hoax, I learn on Wikipedia that "Roger Patterson sold the distribution rights for six figures." And don't forget, that was back in 1967 and showed the thing walking *away* from the camera for only *a few seconds*. Compare that to this afternoon's full frontal display, my God. My *God*! That damn thing wasn't going anywhere. I could've stood there and filmed him in modern hi-def for half an hour! *Note to self: get a hi-def camera.*

After changing my ice bag again and wiping away the blood encrusted on my nostrils and upper lip, I pull up the Patterson Film on YouTube and go over every detail a dozen times. That's no hoax. Only fools who have never seen one up close could think that's a hoax. Plus, the Patterson creature has excellent *tits*—you going to take on that extra architectural burden if you're constructing a realistic suit?

Okay, so these things are real. I guess I'll need to ask Pam for just one more favor then—act as bait. That sounds harsh. I think of all her freaky physical tics and her violent outbursts. I remember her constant habit of swaying back and forth, just like that monster on the ridge. I picture her up on that stage in Kansas City, picking her scabs in front of a crowd of strangers, and it suddenly hits me—she's not bait, she's the Missing Link.

Well, link me in, Little Ticket.

All my energy went to building my shelter of branches and finally crawling inside. It is very simple but I love it. Now I'm burning up and freezing cold. I can't stop the chills. My teeth click together. My belly is boiling F-A-T-A-L stew and I keep squirting valley stream water into my pajama bottoms. My bones are humming low with bad news.

The wild boy might be sneaking across the meadow right this second to help me. Help me. I keep waiting.

No, this is another test. I ate the rabbit. I got sick. But I was only sick in bed. That's not real survival. Now I have to be sick in the wild.

I'll bet he is thinking, *If she wants to be wild, she needs to survive by herself.* Or else he's thinking, *My father will kill me if I go near that girl again.*

How am I supposed to sleep now? It's three in the morning and I'm lying here like a statue in bed. I've spent hours catching up on Bigfoot history. All across North America for centuries, these apes have been terrorizing people.

Okay, okay, I just have to make it to dawn—that's what most reports agree on. I've locked the front door and all the windows. Outside, the only thing I can hear now is a steady rain.

One from 2000, in southeastern Oklahoma, keeps replaying through my mind.

> Too many incidents to mention here, please have someone contact us. My brother is afraid for his family. This creature is getting bolder every time it returns. This thing is huge, walks upright, smells like urine and burned hair-type odor. He repeatedly comes back in the early morning hours after midnight and harasses them until just before dawn. It has on more than one occasion tried to enter their home, slapping the walls and jiggling the doorknob.

Crap, crap, crap, crap. I spring up and double-check all the locks. At least the rain, louder now, is covering any first little sounds of doom. But wait, is that a good thing or a bad thing?

Back in bed, I stare at the ceiling, gradually...gradually relaxing.

I'm body-slammed onto the floor. I guess I body-slammed *myself*, lunging out of bed, and now I can hear why—*there is a Bigfoot tapping at my window!*

I scuttle like a fast crab across the floor, toward the nearest corner, trying not to look at the window.

I have to look. Pam's chalky face, fingers drumming on the glass. *I'm going to kill her.*

But when I switch on the outdoor light and find her crawling up the porch steps, when she climbs into my arms for the first time in six or seven years, I decide to forgive her. The front of her pajamas is covered in blood, faded to brown, which tells me I was right about the baby goat.

And she's a furnace—thermometer reads 104.1.

I've got no ice left because of my nose, so I draw a cold bath and lower her in, pajamas and all. Blood separates from the fabric.

Five days later, I've got her fever under control. Another good sign—she's back to no eye contact and madly swiping and tapping her Kindle screen.

Until this morning, she'd occasionally look up at me, saying without words, *Call the doctor!* That's all I need. Let's call Marlene, too, while we're at it. I've been slaving away with mixed success dispensing antibiotics ibuprofen Diet Cokes almond butter protein shakes bananas crackers cold cloths on forehead PJs washed and fluff-dried good as new.

Our road trip's on hold. Obviously. Dorothy was right—what you've really been looking for has been in your own back yard all along. Or words to that effect. Not sure she was referring to Bigfoot, though.

We're going a different way. My expensive new HD video camera arrived this morning via UPS—*thank you, Kansas City Institute for Cognitive bla bla.*

Once Pam started eating solid food again, I oiled her window and propped it open. I even left her outdoor clothes and jacket draped on the sill. But this morning, they're untouched and she's still wallowing in bed.

I tap her forehead. "Hey, *hey* in there, Little Ticket?" She's pretending to sleep, embracing her Kindle. She does this every time I decide to bring up this particular subject, like she can hear the subject approaching down the hall. "How '*bout* that monster out there, huh? Wish you'd warned me, ha. When did you start *interacting* with him?"

Even after I nab the Kindle—*zoink*—she keeps on pretending. "I've been learning about them. They are gentle with children, so..."

Somewhere deep inside, though, she's listening up—that's her angle. I've heard that people pay closer attention when you whisper. "So I won't stand in your way, all right? Go back up the hill, Pam. Could you put in a positive word for your old dad?" It's called planting the seed. "*Now* I know why you've been going up there all the time. How long have you known that ape for? And you built that statue of your mother's head as some kind of...like an *offering*?"

I caress her cheek and she doesn't even flinch. "I just mean, maybe you could introduce me?"

It must have been beautiful. He probably brought it for me right after the rainy night when I almost died. A gift for lasting so long. Caught in the stream and left on my shelter floor. But now it's covered in flies and pulsing with maggots. I'm still very weak and this sight makes my bones hum low again.

I peel a wedge of bark to fling it out with, far from the doorway. But the smell won't go, so I have to. I lean against the Single Thing, just enjoying the air and sunshine. Find a rocking rhythm that I like. The rhythm of glad to be alive.

When I gave up, that rainy night, I doubted I'd ever see the ridge again. I feel like I've been dead and Hell was ruled by a swollen nose.

Now there's a whole different feeling up here. Lighter. Less pressure.

After resting for an hour, I pick a bouquet of wildflowers. Since this boy lives in nature all the time, he might not like flowers just to look at or to smell. But placing them at the base of the boy's tree makes me smile anyway.

Well, he won't take my gift if I'm just standing here!

I can't go back in my shelter yet, so I cross the meadow to the same bush where I spied on Great White before. Even if I hide perfectly and the boy shows up and finds the bouquet, what are we going to do about his father?

That's a problem we have.

What's your name, Wild Boy?

Another hour goes by before I see the hairless hands of Great

White separating birch saplings to let himself through. He is sneaking up from below, dressed in some kind of fake leaf costume. Is it Halloween time already? No, that's in thirty-eight days away, twenty-two days after my birthday.

He is crawling on his hands and knees. Every once in a while he takes a camera out of his pocket and holds it up to his eye. I've never seen that camera before. He stands on his knees and points it around. It's hilarious to see him with a camera. Trying to copy what my eyes do naturally.

His face is painted a muddy color or else real mud. He looks like soldiers I have seen in movies. His nose is still a little swollen. He keeps on crawling. He thinks he is in a movie.

Of course he doesn't see me. That camera is not going to help him. Seeing happens in the brain and his brain is blind.

What does surprise me is this. I suddenly spot the wild boy across the meadow, lying on his belly way down inside the ferns. All I can see is the top of his head, which would stand out if the ferns were green. He has chosen the brown ferns where I pee. Smart boy, he blends right in. Hope he's not breathing through his nose!

Great White crouches behind a tree. He has binoculars hanging around his neck and lifts them. Scanning back and forth over those brown ferns and my hiding place, too. Without pausing once.

I hear the tapping again and it's coming from the wild boy, but there are no trees. He is making the sound with his tongue.

tock   *tock*   *tocktocktocktock*

Just like I did before. So hilarious!

"Woodpecker," says Great White, nodding to himself.

We punish him with silence, the wild boy and I. For almost five minutes. Great White squirms around. I try to catch the wild boy's eye, in between ferns. He won't look at me. I know exactly how he feels. I notice his eyes notching from side to side. He's taking pictures.

With my own tongue, I make the same sounds. I'm such a good copier that both heads jerk toward me.

Great White doesn't have any idea where it came from, but the wild boy glances directly at me for a quarter second. I can't remember ever wishing someone would keep on looking in my eyes. Then, his head disappears, like a diving seal's, and I hold my breath.

Where will it come up next?

What will he do then?

What's your name?

Suddenly, from a new side of the meadow right across from Great White, comes a complicated bird whistle. I doubt Great White knows that woodpeckers don't produce whistling calls like songbirds. They use percussion or a hard *kwirr* sound. For purposes of communication and to proclaim territory.

After hearing the song a second time, I whistle it myself. Getting all the details right. This stuns the wild boy. Stone silence. My belly sizzles and I clamp both hands over my smile.

Great White can't figure out what to do next. He lets the binoculars fall and swing on their strap. Runs his hand back through his sweaty hair. Rolls his eyes. Mumbles some words to himself.

His mouth slowly falls open when a young tree starts shaking. No wind. Full branches thrashing loudly. Before it comes to a stop, the wild boy crawls like a shot through the low grass. And stands up *in front of a tree*. What kind of tree? clickclickclick. Northern red oak. He's chosen an old one. Wider than his shoulders.

When Great White's eyes are ready to move, the wild boy is standing so straight against his own color that there's nothing to see. Unless you're me.

Oh I love this trick! I love this trick! Right out in the open. So hilarious! Is he showing off for me or does he do this with people all the time just for the fun of it? Either way.

clickclickclickclickclickclickclickclickclickclickclickclick
clickclickclickclickclickclickclickclickclickclickclickclick
clickclickclickclickclickclickclickclickclickclickclickclick
clickclickclickclickclickclickclickclickclickclickclickclick
clickclickclickclickclickclickclickclickclickclickclickclick
clickclickclickclickclickclickclickclickclickclickclickclick
clickclickclickclickclickclickclickclickclickclickclickclick
clickclickclickclickclickclickclickclickclickclickclickclick
clickclickclickclickclickclickclickclickclickclickclickclick
clickclickclickclickclickclickclickclickclickclickclickclick
clickclickclickclickclickclickclickclickclickclickclickclick
clickclickclickclickclickclickclickclickclickclickclickclick
clickclickclickclickclickclickclickclickclickclickclickclick
clickclickclickclickclickclickclickclickclickclickclickclick
clickclickclickclickclickclickclickclick

And that's just his face.

I'm using up all my RAM!

While Great White fumbles with his binoculars, the wild boy raises his left arm and covers this face. Now there's even *less* than nothing to see. The hair on his arm is the exact color of the tree. It hangs like a curtain over his head hair, which is a lighter color.

A few seconds later, I hear footsteps but can't look away from the wild boy. I'm taking all the pictures I can take.

When I check back across the meadow, Great White isn't there anymore. His steps and his cursing are way down the hill already. Then our front door slams.

Now suddenly the trunk of the northern red oak is blank. I should never have looked away! There are no footsteps or slamming doors. Just a large emptiness. My wind feeling around inside it.

Worse, I see the bouquet of wildflowers still at the bottom of the climbing tree.

I flap my hands and slap my head very quickly, trying not to cry.

Wait, what? Something about the flowers. I crawl close. Click back and forth between the pictures of the bouquet at the two different times. It's true! They are all arranged differently!

Now I can finally laugh out loud. So hard it turns into a coughing fit. When did he get the chance to switch the flowers around?

And before putting them back down in their spot, *our* spot, I carefully re-rearrange them again. Sticking my tongue out the corner of my mouth. Black-eyed susans. Shasta daisies. Queen Anne's lace. Clover. I don't put them back the way they were before. I put them in the funniest new way you can imagine.

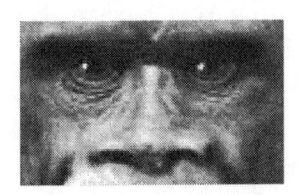

I've got to raise my game and think outside the box. For a problem like this, you can't exactly go find a list of "best practices."

Nothing worth filming up there today anyway, except a weird little tree filled with some type of overactive critters—squirrels? birds?—hidden in the leaves.

I figure I just got lucky that first time. If today *had* been my big opportunity, I'd probably have blown it due to nerves and lack of focus. I'm at a distinct disadvantage.

Time to use my intelligence to turn the tables.

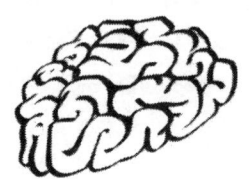

Dawn. I'm back inside my shelter. Had to sleep with my head

in the doorway for fresh air. I'm lying on my belly now, up on my elbows, bouncing my feet behind me and watching a small herd of deer grazing in the meadow.

Last night, I had a filling dinner of grasshoppers and wild leeks. So…wild leeks are an onion-like plant whose leaves and bulbs are edible. You just pull them up and clean the bulbs off with spit. They are crunchy and so much sweeter than regular onions.

Only problem: thirsty again. After my midnight pee, I went around sucking dew for a while. You can get a lot of water out of moss if you don't mind looking stupid. A wild girl doesn't mind.

The deer are beautiful and calm. Too bad. I'm busy sorting through my library of wild boy pictures. These seem more real than the deer. More real than anything in my whole life till today. They make everything else look like two dimensions. The world of people and even the many worlds of Minecraft.

After he covered his face with his arm, I couldn't see his eyes anymore. I took a thousand more pictures of the rest of him. I couldn't tell how tall he was because I didn't know how big the tree was. I just clicked on small squares of him.

After he disappeared, I couldn't look at the pictures yet. I put them aside in a corner of my brain and concentrated on gathering food.

This morning, it's my choice which ones to stare at and which ones to skip till later. Making different categories.

I have decided to start with an ankle. Next, I might try a shoulder, but probably just an elbow. A shoulder is a lot to handle. Definitely an elbow next. Or a knee. There is so much territory to cover. All of it bursting with detail. It could take me weeks! Stop thinking about all that.

The ankle.

It is thick. Not like mine. It does not get any thinner as it goes down toward the foot. It stays the same. Like a pipe. The hairs are thick, too. Close up they look like wire, and not only chestnut colored. There are silvery ones, black ones, blond ones, and even a few coppery-orange ones mixed in there. Some are straight and some are have a soft curl. Those are the blond ones, and they are not as thick. Compared to the wiry ones, I would call them fluffy. But I bet if I held a blond one in my fingers, it would not feel fluffy.

One time, the wild boy shifted his weight and the ankle changed. For half a second. A bulge beneath the hair, low on one side. Just like the knob I have on my own ankle. Then, his ankle went flat again.

There is something else that only appears in a few of the pictures. I think my wind must have tossed some high leaves and let more sunlight slant through. For five seconds, the blond and silver and copper hairs suddenly shine out like they are made of glass.

A hollow thud and the doe sprawls to the ground. The herd scatters.

What just happened?

All I have to do is go back through the pictures my eyes kept taking by themselves while I was back in memory. A rock came like a meteor through the air and struck the doe behind the eye. She lies about twenty feet away. Her legs are so much skinnier than the wild boy's ankle. They are twitching. Her skull is caved in, showing a lot of red flesh. A little bit of white brain.

My belly goes *hk*.

The wild boy swoops in from nowhere. Yanks her off the ground by her neck. Swings her over his shoulder. Because I know how big a doe is, now I can tell how big the boy is. Bigger than I thought. Bigger than Great White.

He is not supposed to come this close to me. I know that he'll get in trouble again. But he played with me yesterday, didn't he?

Today, he is hunting for his family. It must be a large hungry family, if the kids have to hunt too. They grow up so fast out here.

I've only seen the father that one time. I'll bet most of the time he is in a better mood. What parents do is they work together to help their family. They do not yell at each other. They do not quit the family.

I'm sure the wild boy knows I'm here. As usual, he won't look over. Only shows me his broad chestnut back as he hurries with his prize down the fresh trail and into the valley.

Well, well.

I bounce my feet behind me.

Guess that's wildness for you. We go against our fathers. Thanks for the reminder, Wild Boy.

I get up and start collecting rocks. In case mine ever comes back.

I don't let myself rush right over to the flowers at the base of the climbing tree.

When I get there, my arms are full of rocks.

The bouquet is clickclickclickclick untouched and already turning brown.

I just scored big. Got the San Francisco gig to pre-pay us half. Not enough, but there's no shortage of fresh Facebook contacts aching to throw money at us. Our revenue stream is flowing nicely, though none of these gigs will probably ever happen. We'll cross that bridge...

A couple more days and I should have the funds for my next toy. Far more useful than this HD camera—far more maneuverable.

Meanwhile, I just heard from FOX 9 News out of

Minneapolis. They're all hot to come up here to do a live remote spot during their evening newscast! We went ahead and scheduled it, but I've got *no* idea if Pam will even show up on the lawn at 5:30 PM on that day…much less rehearse ahead of time…much less perform before a news crew.

tap tap tap tap tap tap tap

Even though his signal is soft, it wakes me up. Bright moonlight sinks through the loose ceiling of my shelter. I crawl outside. The Single Thing stares at me till I reach back in for my jacket.

I can't see where it comes from but a rock *thwacks* the trunk of the wild boy's climbing tree. Maybe fifty feet away. The rock bounces hard on the ground.

Silence. A far-away owl. I put my jacket on.

Because I'm sleepy, it takes me a minute to catch on.

Oh…my turn!

I grab a rock from my new pile, stand on my knees. Cock my arm and fire at the tree. Not the same solid sound that his made, but I do hit the trunk. Barely. Skimming off the edge.

Before he can take his turn, my next rock strikes the thick middle.

His does, too.

So we're having a contest!

My eyes are clear now. Clear and clicking. I can tell where the wild boy is throwing from. I followed his last rock home. Somewhere in gray-black moon shadows under those leafy branches. Right over there. He's probably much closer to me than we both are to the climbing tree.

Hmmm...that tree trunk has a lot of detail once you start to notice. Under such a fat moon. Two round knotholes, one big, one little. A rough patch of raised bark in the shape of a tilted football. A line running down the left side. Scratched by a bear? Scuffed by an antler?

I choose the little knothole, of course. Almost hit it, first try.

He hits it dead center.

Then, so do I.

Then, he misses by an inch or so.

My chance to win. I drop my rock and sit still.

After two minutes, he makes his bird call. Complicated, like before. I almost call back. Decide not to.

He makes it again, louder this time.

I stretch, yawn, and crawl back inside my shelter.

Soon, I can hear him breathing at the edge of the meadow. In this kind of light, my hand looks like five pearly shells. I let it float up and float back down, glowing. Up and down, again and again, to the rhythm of his breathing.

Till a voice goes *Woooooooooooo!* from deep in the valley. Not the father this time. Calling the wild boy home.

Five nights in a row, we play target practice against the climbing tree. Each time, I cut the game short just when it's getting good. Then, from inside my shelter, I listen to his breathing. Watch my hand.

Night by night, he gets a little bit closer. Always staying till that same high voice says *Wooooooooooo!*

On the seventh and eighth nights, he doesn't come back. I don't sleep.

Number nine, my wind kicks up and there is rain. Too hard to see through or hear through. I can finally sleep.

Tonight, I wake up to the wall of my shelter pressing against my back. I decide it must be my wind, but when that dies down the wall doesn't relax. Then, I hear the breathing at my neck and inhale the richest smell possible. Like all of Earth's blood and soil suddenly brought together.

I expect to freeze stiff. No. I reach back between two branches and touch him. I can't even believe I'm doing this. I've never touched somebody on purpose. I think it's his shoulder. The hair feels exactly like it looks in my pictures.

He jerks back and I hear his footsteps, fainter and fainter and fainter in a light rain.

I know that in the morning, I will wonder if it was a dream. I'm not wondering that now.

I guess I made a big mistake.

We're the same! We can't stand to be touched, either of us.

My skin is burning again. Not with fever this time. And not because I am excited.

From the Internet, I understand that teenagers are supposed to be interested in sex. Not me. Well, not human sex. That makes me really, really sick. I will be a teenager in nine days, but I have never studied human sex or looked at a single picture. I cover my eyes whenever one pops up on the screen.

No, my skin is burning because the Single Thing saw me reaching for the wild boy through the shelter wall.

I am interested in animal reproduction. For species survival.

I jab my elbow against my hip bone over and over. Trying to feel the *twang*. My funny bone's not working tonight. I go into my ball and rock back and forth very fast. Fast like a blur. I hear myself crying like I'm far away.

So...the walnut-sized male blanket octopus will swim up to the much larger female, attach his mating arm to her body with suction cups, and then swim off to die. The female rarely notices as the arm left behind crawls its way around her body, arriving in her gill slit where it waits until her eggs are mature. Another species of octopus, the paper nautilus, will detach his mating tentacle and allow it to swim by itself over to the female.

The elephant's penis can grow to five feet long and is mobile.

It can be used to swat flies away.

C'mon, she seems fine. Hair's kind of a mess, okay, clothes rumpled and filthy, and she's mumbling to herself—but hey, that's my tough old tomboy, self-reliant, autistic savant offspring for you.

I was starting to feel like an irresponsible father, but this afternoon I'm on the porch having lunch and she simply walks across the yard, up the front steps, in the front door, down the hall to her room, and then back outside, dragging her favorite green blanket behind her. Obviously recovered from her illness, moving well, thinking for herself, looking after her own survival needs. It's early October already now, a nip in the air. Leaves turning colors.

I'm actually proud of this kid.

About ten questions flash through my mind. As she passes the remaining surviving goat, she doesn't even pause to pet it, so cutely hopping on the lawn, or to devour it, and then she's long gone again—tip of the blanket vanishing into the forest.

I sigh and take a bite of ham sandwich.

So...how's life among the monsters, Sweetie? Don't do anything I wouldn't do!

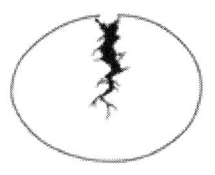

The role of reproduction is to provide for the continued existence of a species. It is the process by which living organisms duplicate themselves.

The wild boy is back for the third night in a row, breathing onto my neck. Wrapping me in those thick layers of smell. It's nice and dark. The moon is almost down to nothing.

I know better than to reach for him again. He does not reach through the shelter wall, either.

But I can tell it's time. He is breathing so close. He can tell, too.

Don't be scared. Don't be scared. Don't be scared.

So...life would not exist on Earth if plants and animals did not reproduce to make their offspring. By reproducing, a living organism can be sure that there is another individual of its own kind to take its place when it dies. There must be a transfer of male reproductive cells from one individual to another, usually into an internal organ or cavity, such as a *cloaca*.

I know I am very young for a person. But in the animal kingdom, I am the perfect right age.

So...male gorillas grow up to 450 pounds, and yet their average penis size is only one and a half inches. From the pictures I took...let me see...that sounds about right.

Nothing to be afraid of. Nothing to be afraid of. One and a half inches.

I'm trembling like when I was sick. I don't know how to do it. I do know the first part. Before I can force my hand to work the snap, there's the worst noise ever heard in the world. Both my hands shoot over my ears.

It's the father roaring at the top of his lungs, again and again, very close by. The roar is high and low at the same time. The high part doing to my head what the rock did to that doe. The low part raking my chest and making the whole shelter tremble around me.

The wild boy is gone.

The roars keep coming.

Please stop. Please stop. Please stop.

Tight in my ball, I picture myself being rolled along by pounding waves, rolled toward a cliff.

Suddenly, moonlight spears through the ceiling. This doesn't make sense because of the sliver moon. When the father stops roaring, a whirring sound takes his place.

The ceiling goes dark again.

I don't care about the shelter. I break open the branches and stick my arms and head up through the roof.

A small spaceship hovers over the trees. Its spotlight is scanning around the meadow. That's strange.

I can't believe what good timing this spaceship has. Saving me from a furious father.

I can't believe what my little life has turned into.

I think the spotlight is looking for them, because it finds them. Stays put. I can see father and son hunched in the tall grass at the edge of the meadow. It looks like the father is trying to choke the wild boy. Then, they raise their arms against the blinding light.

Two curtains of hair this time.

The words "I'm sorry" pop out of my mouth.

Success, right out of the box! And from the comfort of my own desk chair, I got *two* of them like sitting ducks—thirty-seven seconds of crystal clear video, which I'm now replaying obsessively.

Relax, Jim, don't do anything rash like posting it on the Internet for free. If the world wants to see this, it'll cost 'em.

Both apes are gazing straight up into the camera, blinking and exposed, before they finally dive out of frame.

Oh, it was simple. It just required some patience, keeping my window open and an ear out for King Kong. And when he finally broke his silence, boy did he let loose. What could inspire roars like those?

Time to deploy the drone. Since it was delivered, I'd been practicing like a fiend for three days, picking up quite an aviation skill set. Climb to two hundred feet, eyes locked on streaming video portal, locate clearing, descend, avoid trees, sweep target area in a grid pattern.

I was delayed a few seconds when I spotted Helen's head covered by Pam's blanket—*like that hunk needs to be kept warm?*

Anyyyyyway...great job, Little Ticket! Whatever you did up there, it sure worked! Daddy's got what he needs!

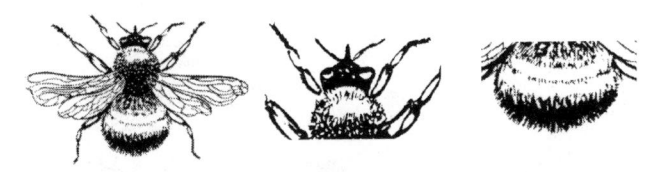

Bad cramps this morning. My personal blood.

So...in females of certain mammal species, menstruation is the cyclical discharge of blood and mucosal tissue from the inner lining of the uterus.

I'm lying curved around the base of the Single Thing. Quilt pulled down over me.

Happy birthday to me.

I'm not feeling very wild this morning. More like a foolish girl who hates her period. Disgusted by what seemed so healthy last night.

All around me, stuck to wildflowers, bumblebees are drying up and dying. And mating. So...in autumn, male bumblebees, called drones, will attach themselves to the much larger females, called queens. At the start of mating, the male will grab onto the queen's thorax to get himself in the correct position, and then he will...

...I will throw up.

Struggling to my feet, I cross to the shelter. Begin repairs to the wall and roof. I'll need fresh leaves and branches.

Before I can choose a tree, I hear last night's whirring sound again.

In daylight, it's not a spaceship anymore. Just some kind of mini-helicopter. Three propellers on top. I stand here watching its level flight as it zips back and forth over the treetops and the open meadow. No, it's not part of nature. But at least it isn't *mating*.

It pauses about twenty feet over my head and just hangs there. I laugh and wave up at it.

"Who are you?"

But I guess this was the wrong thing to do. It tips onto its side, tips the other way, lurches away from me, then quickly spirals down. Crashing into the ground not far from the climbing tree.

It lies in many pieces. Some smoke rises.

Hands on my hips, I feel the blood leaking between my legs.

Everything's ruined.

It's the best way to make sure Pam is okay from a position of safety. I mean, no sense putting *myself* at risk if I might have to mount a rescue operation.

And while we're at it, if I can score even better footage, that's a plus. I already own probably the best Bigfoot video in history, next to the Patterson Film.

Sitting on the porch, flight controller unit on my lap, I operate the joy stick between thumb and index finger.

1. Ascend from lawn
2. Climb quadricopter back up to ridge
3. Visually locate clearing.

4. Dip into clearing
5. Surveil
6. Positive ID—"Oh, there you are!"

Feathery adjustments of the stick bring me down close. She looks good. A little pale. I zoom in. Something remarkable happens—she gazes up at me and laughs. And *waves*! I haven't been allowed to look into her eyes since she changed.

I zoom in even further. I'd forgotten they were this particular shade of blue.

I can read her lips. She says, "Who are you?" *Machines* she will talk to.

The sound of crunching gravel forces me to break eye contact.

It's damn Marlene Stevens again and this time she's got company.

The car stops and both doors open. I have to concentrate on flying. I recover from a little plunge.

"Mr. Manchester."

I sing-song, "Just a miiiinute..."

"*Jim!*"

That voice. I don't want to turn and see the face connected to it...

Youch. Helen has not aged well. There she stands, hands on wide hips, hair gone gray, face loose and sagging compared to the one up there on the ridge, frozen in time.

I return to the video stream in my lap, but this upsets the ladies, who both begin talking at me. I lose control of the drone, diving, but still manage to steer clear of Pam before the monitor goes blank.

Say good-bye to *that* four grand—Helen costing me big, just like the old days.

"Where's my daughter?"

"Well, hello to you, too." I carefully set the console on the table and get to my feet, tightening the belt of my bathrobe. They're both dressed nicely, of course, having had time to prepare.

"I hope this won't be a rerun of those classic therapy sessions where you two gang up on ole Jim." I try to smile as I say this.

The ladies shut their doors but remain by the car.

Helen says, "Marlene tells me Pamela is *living in the woods*?"

"No, she's on one of her nature walks, just up the hill." I gesture casually. "Future Jane Goodall, probably!"

"And she's *sick*?"

"Was sick. *Was*. She's tip-top now. And who do you think nursed—"

"How long has she been up there?"

"How long? What time is it now? Ha. No, not long."

They slowly cross the yard.

"Do you want chairs?" They react as if I'd said *massages* instead of *chairs*. "I'm guessing you saw her online and thought you'd join the fan club."

"What are you talking about?"

"Oh, right. Time to cash in, huh?" I rub my thumb and forefinger together.

"Jim, Marlene called me. I'm not here for a fight."

Oops...shut your mouth. At least some things are still private.

Marlene scratches her face. "Mr. Manchester, we need to take Pamela in for a Sate assessment of her physical and emotional well-being."

I don't say anything.

"Jim? Do you even know that today is her *birthday*."

"...Yes. *Duh*."

"Mr. Manchester, do you still work in town at the..."—our former therapist consults a small notebook—"Radio Shack?"

"No, had to give that up."

"So you do not currently hold a job?"

"Ah, incorrect. I've started my own business. You know, as a *single parent of a special needs child*, I can't exactly leave Pam with anyone."

"I see. What sort of business?" She's poised to take notes.

"Oh, we're making ends meet, and then some. I can tell you this much, she and I are working on a major project together. As far as the details, those are way too technical for—"

Marlene points to the fallen tree. "*There* she is, Helen. Pamela dear, can you—"

Helen raises her hands to the sides of her head. "Oh my God! *Look* at her!"

Pam's face crumbles like I haven't seen since she was a baby. On her way back up through the trees, running, she makes a new type of bellowing sound.

I find a quiet pool in the stream. First, I drink and drink. Then, I sit and I wash my face and my hair. Moss for a sponge. I am washing the rest of me. To start a new life, I left my dirty clothes up on the ridge.

I've still got my green quilt with me.

I'm letting the water swirl my blood away. The cold feels so good on my cramps. I'm not worried about being naked because so are they.

Where are they? What's his name?

I splash water in front of my face once, twice, three times.... Sunlight sparkles through and plays with my eyes. Stars and jokes. Stars and jokes!

Eighty-five...eighty-six....

I am going for a thousand and then I will wrap myself in my quilt.

I was going home for a hot bath, some pads. Change of clothes. To sleep once in my bed. I should have known better. That's not what a wild girl does! I was weak and lazy!

When I heard voices, I hid behind the fallen tree.

"Oh my God! *Look* at her!" What I did last night at my shelter turned her hair all gray. That's why she came back. She came back because of what I did.

Two hundred eight...two hundred nine...two hundred ten...

She knows what I did even though I draped the quilt over her eyes.

After she said, "*Look* at her!" I ran to the ridge and kicked the Single Thing. It took nine kicks to tip it over.

I stood there staring at it.

Five hundred forty-two...five hundred forty-three...

There are animals down here. Frogs at the edge of the pool. Mosquitoes in the air. Mayflies rowing on the silver surface, taking quick turns. Five different kinds of birds, including a great blue heron, who is fishing two pools downstream.

And fish.

Six hundred ninety-eight...six hundred ninety-nine...seven hundred. Too cold. My wind wrinkles the surface of the water. I wade out. I pull the quilt around me and run in place.

Even though I'm far down, the valley goes even deeper. Below me, the stream zigzags back and forth, cutting into the earth. I have to follow.

I need to tell the wild boy what today is.

Sobbing, Helen removes a cake from the back seat of the car. *Complete with candles—that's rich. How ya gonna light 'em?*

But she sets off with it into the woods, immediately tripping on a root, and the whole thing goes spat.

After five or ten minutes of aimless interaction—including a period of exaggerated group attention to the remaining baby goat—we all sit in silence on my porch.

"Well," says Marlene, jingling her keys, "I'll leave you two alone for a while."

Helen nods, using a tissue.

"I do need to inform you, Mr. Manchester, that I have Judge Amenta on call. I hoped it wouldn't come to this, but I will be back in two hours with a court order stipulating that the child be remanded into temporary State custody. If you are not able to turn her over, I'm afraid the system will kick in at the next level. Tomorrow morning, officers of the law will be here, prepared to carry out the order."

Half of me is thinking, *Shit shit crap shit, I totally blew it this time*. The other half is like, *Good luck, officers of the law! I won't mention the eight-foot ape man up there, but if you shoot him on my property, I will legally own the body. Remand that, bitch.*

"Um, is there any way," asks Helen, "for me to have her for a while?" She puts a hand out toward me. "I mean, just during the...evaluation period."

"Unfortunately, no. You do not have custody of your daughter and don't have legal standing in the current matter. Mr. Manchester, do you understand the terms I have just laid out to you?"

In my head, I reject plenty of snappy comebacks and end up just tipping an imaginary cap.

Annoyingly, almost as soon as Marlene's car disappears, I find myself losing my hard edge toward Helen—she's just so damned sniffly and apologetic. Plus, the therapist has already lapped up my finest hatred for herself.

Obviously, my ex wants to get some things off her chest. Do I have to listen?

"I'm remarried, Jim. We live in St. Paul. My husband is

Clifford and we have a five-year-old son named Tucker." *Poor Tucker. Poor Clifford.*

"Okay..."

"I need to admit that I am not proud of what happened here with us. I was not emotionally equipped. I don't know which was worse for who I was back then, you or the autism. Clearly, I couldn't cope with either."

She waits for me to respond, then says, "After Pam...turned *in*, you know, I felt lost in space. You were lost too and couldn't be there for me. I mean we couldn't be there for each *other*."

Waits.

"Well...so..."

Four thousand bucks.

"I'm ashamed of what I put Pam through and I know I can never make up for seven years of absence."

"You took her *cat*."

Weeping. *Score.*

"Benjamin was the only one I could connect with. We finally had to put him down last year."

More weeping.

"Well, we've been doing fine out here, Helen. In fact, we're tip-top."

She dabs at her eyes and mops up around her nose. "Jim, she contracted rabbit fever and now she's missing in the wilderness."

I raise my index finger.

"For what it's worth, I kept meaning to get in touch. You know how when time goes by between people, the more that goes by the harder it gets, like this...wall of time?"

"Want a Diet Coke?"

She shakes her head.

"Think I'll get one." While inside, I trot to my office and watch my thirty-seven seconds of Bigfoot footage again. I keep noticing new details, like how the bigger one's head is so much more cone-shaped than the smaller one's. I can't believe I got *two* of them in one shot and had the chance to really zoom in on their faces. Nobody in the world has video or pictures of even *one* face this clear. When they blink up into the searchlight, just before they cover their faces with their arms, I can see that their mouths are set lower than people's—more space between nose and upper lip.

I crack the seal on my Diet Coke bottle and replay the very beginning. The drone's searchlight sweeps back and forth over the ground and for a split second strikes the pair of apes, crouched in the tall grass, before it moves on. At the time, I remember quickly aiming it back and locking in for the money shot, but during that first glimpse, on the first pass, they're in a different posture. I can't quite figure it out. The big one is doing something to the smaller one, but the camera's shaking too much to tell. I'll need to teach myself some fancy video-enhancement tricks.

When I sit back down on the porch, Helen has this far-away look in her eyes, gazing past me into the woods. "Anyway, I've been educating myself about autism, Jim. There's so much to learn. I've read probably a hundred books. Did you know this condition actually has ancient roots? In the Middle Ages, when a child suddenly changed like ours did, people thought it was because they'd been stolen and replaced. Literally *switched*. They called these children 'fairy changelings.'"

She still talking? I'm imagining myself on Jimmy Fallon. I've decided to give him the exclusive first rights, the world premiere of my video, and now Jimmy's asking me to "set up the clip," like it's from a motion picture. Ha!

Helen clears her throat, then helps herself to a sip of my Diet Coke. "Snatched away to live in the woods. In *Outside Over There*, Maurice Sendak has this one amazing line I remember: 'So the goblins came. They pushed their way in and pulled the baby out, leaving another all made of ice.' Isn't that amazing?"

"Kind of."

"I just found it comforting, that's all. To learn that Pam is part of this long, well-known tradition. That families have been struggling with this for hundreds or maybe thousands of years. There's a famous case in the 1700s of Victor, 'The Wild Boy of Avalon'"—

Oh yeah, Helen's air quotes—how I've missed you.

—"who lived his entire childhood alone in the woods in France. Before he left the household, he showed definite signs of autism, although of course they didn't have that diagnosis back then."

Her excited flush tempts me to spill the beans about my daughter's stardom, holding a thousand people in the palm of her hand in Kansas City. But then I shake myself, remembering what Helen did to us.

I want to scrounge up some new topic.

"Then there's Amala and Kamala, two 'feral' girls from India who were supposedly 'raised by wolves.' But, Jim, that turned out to be a myth, just a way of explaining their animal-like behavior."

I hack it to pieces! The snake segments curl and whip on their own. Daring me to keep going. Now they're all diced and steaming on a flat rock. I used to dice onions and tomatoes like this in the kitchen. Garter snakes are easy to catch in the fall. Sluggish on a chilly night.

I knew this propeller blade would come in handy. I grabbed it from the crashed helicopter on the hill. After I kicked the Single Thing down. Poor helicopter. Trying to make friends with me. Why did it have to crash?

Here in the stream, I've got all the water for a lifetime. The only problem is food. This snake tastes delicious. I gather the paste with my fingertips. You never know what will taste how. No need to spit out the bones, either. That's how sharp this blade is. I've wrapped a thick rhubarb leaf around the handle.

On my way deeper into the valley, I quickly recognized the spot where I'd found Knees. Not because of blood but because I have a photographic memory. I never knew I had this till Great White started making me do shows and I had to listen and listen to his boring speeches. And listen.

Then my journey got pretty rough. More and more rocks to climb over. I saw an owl in a tree, a large barred owl. She looked at me struggling along inside my quilt like "You're kidding." But I kept on climbing down.

At last, I reached to the bottom. The stream is thin here, and then it travels underground. I thought I'd run into the wild family, waiting in a circle to welcome me.

That's not what happened. That was ridiculous. There is nothing down here, nothing but rocks and pine trees. And snakes. I see a second one, fatter and longer this time. Click a picture of where it goes. I'll eat you later.

So…as winter approaches, a bear will gorge itself, eating more than three times the amount of calories it does in the summer. These calories turn into excess fat that fuels the bear's body during hibernation.

After two more snakes, I drink. My pee steams like diced snake. I find a patch of moss down between two rocks and lie in the tight squeeze inside my quilt. Like a cocoon. My only friend. I miss my shelter on the ridge but this quilt is warm and puffy. I can make a kind of pillow by rolling up the edge. What a good friend.

I picture myself all curled up inside a bear's belly. This warms me.

I don't sleep at all, but when I open my eyes, it's suddenly dark. I mean pure black. I can't tell if my eyes are clicking, because every picture is the same. My wind has trouble reaching me here, low inside low, but when it does it's got stone inside it, so I tuck my nose back under my quilt.

I leave an ear out for tapping, knocking, rock-throwing. Whatever they feel like. Whatever you feel like. Even yelling at me to go home, that would be fine. That would make sense. I just want to know they are still here. And for them to know I'm sorry. I understand what I did wrong. I tried to join them before I was ready. I need to prove myself first. Who does she think she is? Little hairless girl!

After half an hour, I poke my face out into the cold again and go *tock tock tock tock* with my tongue. Can they hear me down in this squeeze? *tock tock tock tock tock tock tock tock*

The way the father roared last night still slams my chest. It would be funny if what I did on the ridge made that family go...and *her* come. She came all the way back just because of what I did. She waited seven years till I did it. Then, she said, "Oh my God. *Look* at her!"

They might be in next valley, or fifty miles away. Who does she think she is? We've got plenty of world.

Sheriffs Rooney and Fiske look way too young. They pull their official shiny white squad car alongside Marlene's and step out. We shake hands all around.

"Don't you guys usually wear sidearms?"

"Not on a 964, sir," says Fiske, "domestic child recovery." They chuckle together. "Wouldn't want to freak out the kiddos."

I see... Well, what about "child recovery with prehistoric hard-ass involved"? That would be a...what...a -964?

"Let me confirm," Marlene says, "that you do not have Pamela Manchester ready to be remanded into temporary State custody."

I flash her a peppy thumbs-up. She writes in her little notebook, shaking her head. I would respect her more if she drew a picture of my thumb instead.

Rooney asks, "When and where was your daughter last seen, Mr. Manchester?"

Helen chimes in, "We had her yesterday morning at about eight, right behind that fallen tree. Then, she took off up the hill there. She can't be too far."

"Yes," I add, "she comes and goes all the time. Just a tomboy enjoying her...expanded back yard." I spread my arms wide.

"Keep in mind she is profoundly autistic. She will *not* respond when called."

"Yes, we *have* read your report, Doctor Stevens," Fiske assures her.

While they start blathering on about tactics, I slip inside to my computer. I decided overnight—somewhere inside my own tactical brain—to post just the first ten seconds of my footage on YouTube. I titled it "Two Bigfoots in Minnesota Woods! Real! Must See!" It took about two minutes to upload—such a simple process for a turning-point in history. The clip includes my searchlight locating them and then the two faces blinking up from a distance. At the exact moment I start to zoom in, it cuts off—*ha, take that, panting viewers!* For the description, I wrote, "The rest of this video shows their faces in extreme close-up. Will sell to the highest bidder. Only serious offers considered. Bidding to start at $10,000. PM me through this YouTube channel." Of course I didn't use my name. I started a new channel called Victory123.

So far, the clip hasn't caught on. Only 314 views. Two idiots actually "disliked" it! So many bogus Bigfoot videos out there, distracting the world, it's hard to recognize the genuine article.

Only a matter of time…

I sit back with my hands behind my head and let out a deep breath. It's a warm day so I have my office window open. The squawk of the sheriffs' walky-talkys fades up into the woods. I'd probably be following them, out of pure curiosity, if only they were carrying elephant guns. Sounds like the two are separating now. *Bad idea, fellas.*

Helen and Marlene talk quietly on the front porch, probably expecting me to join them, offer them breakfast or at least coffee.

I open Google Earth. Time to survey the territory. It does strike me as weird that I've never done this before, but then again, I've had no reason to. Nothing but wilderness around here—just more and more damn nature. But flying that drone got me intrigued.

Turns out the valley beyond the ridge is actually a sharp ravine. The elevation falls from 1438 ft. on top to 212 in a hurry. A girl could get lost down there. Bigfoot could stay undiscovered down there!

The deed to the property is in a kitchen drawer. As I unfold it, I nod to Helen through the screen door. She's rocking nervously in my chair, reminding me of our daughter. Her face looks bloodless.

What do you know, that ravine is *mine*. Well, technically it's Helen's. Back when I bought her out of the house, going broke, I wound up with two acres and she kept the other hundred and eight. All inherited from her grandparents. She doesn't care. She's too square and bookish to own a deep ravine.

Back at my desk, I find that "Two Minnesota Bigfoots" suddenly has 1123 views. Yes, it's happening! I check my PMs—no bidding war quite yet…the calm before the storm.

I'm about to reply to some of the more good-natured comments, explaining how I managed to obtain the footage, when I'm startled by the voice of a sheriff in the yard. "Tom, do you copy? Tom."

Through the window, I see the women cross to him. No, he doesn't have Pam in custody—my girl's way too slippery. He lowers his walky-talky. "Rooney's out of range."

clang! clang! clang! clang!
Propeller blade against rock. What a high and perfect sound. *clang! clang! clang! clang! clang! clang! clang! clang! clang! clang! clang! clang! clang! clang! clang!*

Instead of getting an answer from the wild boy, I hear...radio static. That's the last thing I want to hear. I duck back between the two rocks, into the squeeze. Peek out.

A man in a brown and gold uniform is handing himself from tree to tree down the valley wall. Some kind of policeman. Great White would never be able to do that.

When he reaches the stream, the policeman stands there catching his breath. Looking around.

"Pamela!" This surprises me. "Pamela Manchester, was that you signaling for help? I heard you. Can you hear *me*? Are you hurt, Honey?"

The man lifts his cap and smooths back his hair. He drinks from a pea green container and clips it back onto his belt.

Just then, he doubles over and looks like he wants to throw up. He even goes down on one knee.

I feel it too. Something in the air. Some type of heavy rumble hitting the back of my head and my shoulders. Hollowing out my belly. Going *wawawawawa* against the stone surfaces by my ears.

It's too tight in the squeeze to turn around. I have to crawl out and hide behind another rock. Now I can scan the other side of the valley clickclickclick till I spot him partway up.

The father.

The sun isn't down here yet so he's almost invisible in pine shade. I had to take nine different pictures of that same spot to make sure it was him. Now that I know, he's easy to watch. The valley wall is so steep he's not really that far away. Squatting on a rock ledge. Hanging over us.

Without even opening his mouth, the father fills and empties his huge chest. Then, the next wave crashes over me. Why can't I hear it? Oh yeah!

So…low-frequency sound, or infrasound, is below what humans can hear. It is used by a variety of large mammals, such as buffalo, giraffes, tigers, hippos, etc. Elephants, for example, use this kind of sound as a private means of communication across miles of savannah. They "hear" it through their feet. And blue whales can project their calls one hundred miles away through open ocean. Infrasound can also penetrate flesh and bone, disturbing the central nervous system of its target. Lions have been documented to paralyze prey, such as antelopes, with their roar.

I want to learn how to do that, too!

I peek at the policeman. He is trying to climb back, tree to tree, the same way he came. This time, he goes very slowly, slipping on dirt and dead leaves. Sometimes losing his cap.

Two more shiny sheriff cars arrive, sliding to a stop on either side of the first. Fiske has called for back-up. Three men and a woman—and these four *are* armed.

Now we're getting somewhere. I own the ravine, so feel free to monster-hunt in there.

As they begin discussing the search for Rooney, the man himself suddenly emerges, stumbling, disoriented, soaking wet, face literally greenish. He sits hard up against the fallen tree.

"I think it's...the girl. She's *down* there. I heard her banging metal against stone. I got close, but then I felt sick all of a sudden. I don't know what's wrong with me. I've been walking in circles..."

The baby goat bounds up to him, butting his shins.

"Okay, okay!" Marlene announces. "This is making sense." She strikes a pose of authority, enclosing the group within her arms. "Autistic children have a tendency to repeatedly hit objects together. This is because they find comfort in rhythm, due to the bla bla bla bla bla bla..."

Know what else has that tendency? Hey, I've done my research—"Bigfoot is a highly percussive species." I need to become an expert pretty quick, by the time I go on Jimmy Fallon. A walking encyclopedia like Pam, but only covering this one topic. Turns out there's not a whole lot of information to digest, anyway. Bigfoot has basically stumped the human race...until now. Lots of hoaxes and harebrained theories, that's about it. There's even some Texas veterinarian who's going around claiming that "they're a type of people." *Oh really? Wonder what neighborhood you grew up in, Lady.*

I can't wait to race back to my computer and the bidding war. But I'll admit we've got a bit of a situation brewing here on the lawn. Helen's getting hysterical, a condition I remember only too vividly. *Poor Clifford. Poor little Tucker.*

"I have to go up there! I *have* to!" she proclaims. "I must have frightened her away with my reaction yesterday."

The female sheriff—her tag says DiMarco—drapes an arm across Helen's shoulders and speaks gently. "I'm sure she forgives you."

"It's just...she caught me so off guard."

"I know, I know, dear. We're absolutely going to need you once we locate her, to…close the deal. Here's a walky-talky. Please hold this and stand by."

Helen accepts it with a healthy sigh, returning DiMarco's confidence and back-pats.

Fiske, feeling a little better, has decided to play with the baby goat after all.

Marlene says, "We are dealing here with a unique case that calls for extreme patience and flexibility. I have worked intensively with Pamela over an extended period of time"—*not so fast, Slick; you met with us once a week for exactly five months long, long ago*—"and we need to understand that the forest has become her sanctuary. We represent the chaos of the outside world trying to invade and take control. I believe she will go to any lengths to avoid us, and with this in mind I propose…"

Here's another fun fact I plan to trot out on Jimmy Fallon— "Bigfoots avoid human contact better than any other creature on Earth. If they did not, given their great size, they would have been discovered centuries ago. But we still do not understand exactly *how* they manage this remarkable feat."

Before Marlene has finished educating her students about the subtle ways of autism and the indirect strategy that must be employed out there today, how the pursuers should pretend to be fascinated by objects in *nature* and not focus on Pamela herself, how this may draw her attention and potentially bla bla bla…the five sheriffs back away, politely thanking her, and melt into the woods. Wait, recount, six. No longer greenish, Rooney's up and eager for further humiliation. "Follow me!" he shouts, charging ahead.

They don't invite Marlene. She stands at the tree line snapping pictures with her cell phone until the uniforms disappear. *Expecting to write a major paper about our "unique case" here, Doc? Hoping for a helping of fame and fortune? Get in line!*

By the goat-house, she rejoins Helen, who grips the walky-talky like it's a bar of gold. "Shouldn't you be up there with them, Jim?"

"Me? Ha, no! I'm the *last* one they need in the party. Pam's made a science of knowing my tricks and steering clear of me. She'd smell me coming from a hundred yards. No, I've got a ton of..."—thumbing toward the front door—"...you know, work never stops for family!"

Back at my screen, I find that my video has exploded—12,000+ views in just under two hours, showing how hungry the world is for the real McCoy. And I've got a first bid. $200. $200? *Moron—I said $10,000!*

What's this? Some video nerd with no life has already posted an enhancement—"Minnesota Bigfoot Slowed and Stabilized." But I'm actually glad because now the image doesn't shake around and you can see better what's going on in the early sequence. The big one has the smaller one...*by the throat!* You can clearly see the massive hand wrapped around the other one's neck, making the eyes go wild with anger or surprise or pain or—who knows, maybe nothing. I guess these apes will just lash out at each other for no reason.

"Please please please please please please please please pleasepleasepleasepleasepleasepleasepleaseohpleasewildboy pleasepleasepleasepleasepleasepleasepleasepleasewhatsyourna mepleasepleasepleasepleasepleasepleaseohpleasewildboy..."

Hugging my knees, I hum a nonsense tune to the words "please." I want my quilt. I left it back there, tucked inside the squeeze. I am so naked.

After the policeman left the valley, the father came down from his ledge and I thought maybe he was going to kill me right then.

I dropped my propeller blade and raised my hands. I told him I would never carry it anymore. He didn't even bother to look at me. He just turned and walked away.

And that's when I noticed his legs, how he stepped over these great big rocks like they were bowling balls. They come up to my waist and higher.

I did my best to keep up with him, crashing and falling and getting up. Holding my sore breasts as I ran. Calling, "Sorry! Sorry! Sorry! I'm sorry!" Till I lost him in the glare of the sun.

I think what I need to do is sit down in the stream again. I need to splash water in the light. Stars and jokes. I need to splash it! I need to splash it! But the water is somewhere beneath me now. Underground. So unless I want to dig, all I can do is sit here and rock. Flap my hands by my head. Slap my head.

What is your name, Wild Boy? Did you get punished? Me, too. I'm being punished. The sun feels so good on my back and shoulders.

Tickle tickle. When I look down, my light red friends are crawling over the tops of my feet. You! Underneath my feet, I see what the problem is. Tunnels and tunnels. Another colony. Ants are carrying their eggs to safety.

I don't touch the egg-carriers. Some others I put back on my knee. The scab's too healed for them to taste. They just wander off. I pinch them to my lips for breakfast.

"We've located her. She *has* been located." DiMarco's voice. She's come back to get us. I quickly find out they haven't exactly *seen* her. "We heard her shouting 'Sorry!' So we think she feels badly about what she's put everyone through and *wants* to be rescued."

Marlene clears her throat. "I'm not sure about your analysis there, Sheriff. Regardless, it's at this point that we must apply utmost caution and an appropriate technique, or else—"

"Let's go get her!" Helen yanks DiMarco into the woods by the arm. "This might be our best chance."

I could just let them have their fun and stay behind, basking in Internet glory and watching my stock rise. But I have to say I'm kind of interested, especially with Marlene left here fuming. Not to mention Bigfoot. Daylight footage would be the cherry on top, to go with my drone footage. I retrieve my HD video camera from inside.

Marlene has trouble with the first hill, but I don't offer my hand.

On the ridge, Helen is staring at her own giant head, which has been toppled over by Mr. Goliath. *Poor Pam. Note to self: fix that for her.* Nearby, there's a pile of branches and all her dirty clothes. Now I'm getting nervous. What's he done to her? They are supposed to be *gentle* with children.

Marlene hurries to Helen's side, butting in between her and DiMarco. "I wouldn't read too much into this. These children, such *gifted artists*, will often create exact replicas of objects in their world."

"She made me just to knock me down."

"Don't forget, they heard her saying she's *sorry*."

"To destroy me. She hates me that much. And I deserve—"

"See, that's precisely the wrong—"

"We're wasting time!" I suggest, heading into the ravine.

In five minutes, we four join the five male sheriffs, all gathered on a kind of earthen tier overlooking a boulder field. They've got their eyes turned away and I suddenly see why. Pam's balled up and rocking below us—with not a stitch of clothing.

Marlene documents it with her phone. Before I can knock it out of her hand, Helen shouts, "Pamela!" and starts to climb down.

Marlene grabs her arm. "No!"

Pam looks up, unfolds herself, and disappears in a precocious flash behind a boulder. I can breathe again.

"You see," explains Marlene, "that's why the blunt approach will never work." She faces the group with barely concealed educational pleasure. "As I said, the only way to—"

"Pamela, it's me, your *mother*! Honey, I came back to see you! I'm sorry about yesterday! And about..."

"There's enough of us," Sheriff Rooney points out, "to surround her and close in."

"That I can*not* allow!" Marlene makes a corralling gesture with her hands. "Such an experience would traumatize the child permanently. What we need to do at this point is to stop paying attention to her."

"Pamela! Honey!"

What in the hell?

It's Helen's voice again but now coming from the opposite side of the ravine.

"Pamela! Honey!" Again. Goddamned dead ringer.

Helen kind of launches herself against me. "Jim, she's throwing it right back in my *face*."

"No, it can't be her," I say.

"Is the whole *valley* making fun of me?"

Everybody is mystified. Everybody but Marlene. "People, people. What we are witnessing here is a rather common phenomenon known as *echolalia*. Autistic children will copy, or 'echo,' the speech of others."

"But the girl is down there and this came from across...over there somewhere." Sheriff Fiske points. His colleagues nod. We all stare dumbly at the trees across the way.

Marlene piles on more information. "The acoustics inside a narrow space like this are often deceptive."

"Pamela! Honey!" It's much too loud, anyway. But apes can't

talk.

They are coming down.
The wild boy will help me. He tried to scare them by copying her voice. Good copying, Wild Boy! I wave to him where he's blending into the valley wall, watching me where I hide. I'm naked. But we're both naked, so.
The people will be here. How will he help me?
Suddenly, I get a picture in my head: a pond. And it comes with a direction, too. I rip some ferns out of the ground to cover up with, top and bottom. Then, I run.
"There she goes!" They're calling out to me but I won't listen. I just need to find that pond. No more rocks here. Now it's a marsh. Now my feet are landing in water, sucked into mud. Sawtooth grasses scrape my legs.
I see it! A round pond just like the picture.
I wade up to my thighs, then sit down *plunk*. Almost up to my chin. There are frogs at the edge. And mayflies for them to eat. I want to sit and watch them eat. Watch them live their lives. But the people are forming a circle around me. Speaking words I try to push away it'sokaypamelawearen'tgoingtohurtyouthisisfor yourownsafetyno!thisisnotthewaytoapproachher!youallneedtop ullbackimmedieatelywehavetotakethepressure*off*Iwon'tbeaparty totreatingherlikeananimal

splash! splash! splash! splash! splash! splash! splash! splash! splash! splash! splash! splash!
The sunlight is sharper and yellower out here than it was back at the stream. It bounces off the drops. Stars and jokes. Stars and jokes for my eyes. what'sgoingtohappenowpamelaokayiswe're

justgoingtohelpyououtofthewaternowpamhoneyit's*mom*I'msoso rry

splash! splash! splash! So pretty so pretty so pretty it bounces off the drops and—

WHOOOSH in the middle of the pond. The father rises there. Water rushing off his head and shoulders. He shakes more off like a towering dog. Up this close, he is wider than the goathouse. I can't tell how tall he is because how deep is the pond? He's standing on the bottom. The surface comes to his hairy belly. I know I'm not good at telling faces, but he doesn't look angry or anything like that. Just plain sure of himself. The top of his head is shaped like a dome, not flat like mine.

I'm pretty surprised to see him. But not half as surprised as the people. I don't scream or run backward like them. I stay still and watch him sway back and forth, back and forth, making waves.

I don't fall over backward and get up and fall over again and keep screaming. Like the people. They are fun to watch.

The father doesn't look at me. So I also watch him. I understand he won't hurt me. Last time he had the chance he didn't. I feel safe. He doesn't even roar. He doesn't need to.

The frogs are pretty interested, too. He's got a dark beard I've never noticed before. Now it's wet and hanging straight down. Both hands are under water till he lifts one out to wipe his eyes.

Still running backward, Great White takes his camera out of his pocket but drops it into the marsh. He starts fishing for it but then decides to change direction. He's coming back for me. Stepping slowly, boots going *thwuck* every time he pulls them from the mud. Both hands stretch out toward me. To calm *me* down?

I'm laughing and laughing when the father does roar. It's the loudest thing ever. The frogs jump in. My head goes numb. Great White turns and runs, grabs *her* hand. They escape like little children back up the valley wall with the others.

Everyone collapses onto the yard—everyone except Marlene. Without a word, she simply gets into her car and drives away, tires actually spitting gravel. *Can't stand the heat, eh? Doubt we'll be seeing much of you from now on.*

The rest of us stare into space for an untold length of time—ignoring the cries of the goats, who need food—until the sheriffs finally shake their heads clear enough to decide they should probably check in with headquarters. Off they go, too.

So it's back down to Helen and me now, down to the nub. She's in shock, almost mute, so I put her to bed in Pam's room. I've seen the creature before, so I'm less in shock than relieved to know I'm not insane.

Nobody spoke the whole way back through the woods. It was like some kind of death march—for them, humiliation and disbelief, for me, missing out on the greatest video footage the world will never see. At least I've still got the drone clip.

I finally drag myself into the office. On YouTube, my video is up past 123,000 views, but before I can check in to the bidding war, another video catches my eye in the right-hand column—"Minnesota Bigfoot Hoax!!!"

Oh really?

This guy is breaking down just the first three seconds, rocking it forward and backward. "Here," he points out, "we can see figure #1 helping figure #2 on with his fake head! We can't see the head being *put on*, but the hoaxer made the fatal mistake of showing the *end* of the process, where the man who's already in his suit is connecting the other one's suit together, fitting the head piece to the body piece at the neck. Right here, plain as day! You can even see the fingers moving a little"—back and forth, back and forth goes the clip—"to work the buttons or snaps or zipper...or whatever it is. Of course, the dumbass filming this realizes his mistake and takes the camera off them till they're ready. Whoops ha ha! Sorry...too late! Now look at him sitting there blinking up at the camera all innocent, like, 'Hoaxer? Who...me?' Blink blink blink...ha ha ha ha ha! Nice try, Victory123...*not!* Case closed!"

Over the next couple of hours, the Internet explodes with agreement and ridicule, Google pointing me to dozens of Bigfoot websites dedicated to destroying others and promoting themselves.

I keep picturing my camera lying dead among swamp reeds.

I expect the father leave the pond. And then, after his dome head disappears back under the water, I expect him to come up for air.

It's really quiet here. Sometimes, a ripple on the surface. Just a minnow or mayflies. Or my wind chills my neck so I dip lower. I know if I get out, I'll be way colder. My wind pats my cheek, making sure I'm okay. I'm okay.

I kind of wish the father would grab my ankle like Great White used to do in the city pool, when I was little.

One by one, around the edge, the frogs show up again. "Did he drown himself?" they ask me.

When crows call from far away, I start shivering. My teeth are clacking together. The sun has gone behind a cloud. clickclickclickclickclickclickclick. Pictures of the valley wall show me that where the wild boy was before...watching me, showing me the pond...he isn't anymore.

The water spreads out clean and calm in front of me. Where is everybody hairy? Should I give up on being wild? Will I ever be warm and cozy again? What will I do with my life?

Luckily, because I am a natural winner, the rage and depression subside pretty quickly. Now it's back to Facebook, where "Kid Genius!" is still a sizzling commodity, and where the offers keep getting more generous—Book it! Book it! Book it! Book it!

Over the next several hours, my bank account swells as conferences and universities eagerly ante up through PayPal—all on the strength of the thumbprint performance.

And then, while I'm playing Angry Birds, an idea hatches that is so good it rescues my life in a snap.

The *new* new gizmo is twenty-nine thousand bucks! I order it on Amazon. Just go ahead and order it—*can do*.

Two minutes later, a news story breaks on the CNN homepage.

DRAMATIC NEW BIGFOOT VIDEO
DEFINITIVE PROOF?

> A psychologist who gives her name only as Marlene S. has come forward with a startling piece of cell phone footage that she claims to have obtained this very morning in an isolated valley somewhere in the United States...

I believe I have just enough ketamine hydrochloride left. I could stir it into a pint of Cherry Garcia. To churn these suicidal thoughts, I keep refreshing Marlene's brand new YouTube channel, where her views climb five thousand per minute.

I have to admit, it's spectacular. The clip would never have hit the mainstream, instantly like this, if it were not. But I can't even use it to back up my ridge footage, because Marlene's refusing to identify the location. I keep focusing on Pam's head, which looks tiny in one corner of the frame, as though floating on the pond water.

Helen wanders in and sees the video before I can gather my wits and close the screen—big mistake.

On the other side of the pond, I find a higher place. A field of wild leeks.

Going back to retrieve the quilt was almost as bad as waking up on that airplane. So cold, like death! But now, I eat a big crunchy lunch of leeks, saying "crunchy lunchy...crunchy lunchy."

Then, I tip over into the grass. Make a pillow with the edge of the quilt. Down here inside these stalks, the sunlight is white instead of yellow. I blink in this milky world, missing the goat-house.

The sound of splashing wakes me up. I want to splash, too! I want to splash, too! The wild boy won't look at me, but as soon as I sit up and rub my eyes, he stops his splashing. It's dusk already. He's all under water except for his head and shoulders. Just like I used to be. Before I can think of what to say or what to do, he sinks below the surface, making a quick little whirlpool.

I scratch my face.

That's what your father did.

You want me to follow you?

When I dip my foot in, those bones ache. The last thing my body wants to do is lose this quilt again. No, the last thing my body wants to do is lose this quilt and then go into cold water again.

Back among the wild leeks, wrapped up tight, I rock and rock and try to decide to ignore him, like I did before, up on the ridge.

I can't sit here forever. I can't go home. I can't even go to the ridge, or they'll catch me forever. What is between forever and forever? I *twang* my funny bone against my hip while the light drains from the sky over the valley.

To calm her, I sit Helen down and fill her in on every piece of history she's missed. When I get to our daughter's recent sleeping habits, that finally does the trick—she gathers Pam's sheets, pillows, clothing, even her piggy bank and Kindle, and heads straight out to the goat-house herself.

While I'm checking the tracking information on my UPS delivery, an email appears from FOX 9 News, wishing to confirm the live remote spot for tomorrow afternoon from our back yard—*completely forgot!*

I send my sincere regrets…

Not sincere enough, apparently, given their explosive reaction.

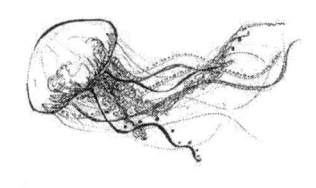

Feet first and all at once, that's the only way. Or I'd chicken out. And where the wild boy disappeared last night it's too deep to wade in step by step anyway.

I tread water for a minute, remembering last night's long dream...a slide show of extinct animals. I could tell from a kind of vibration that these animals used to live right here in northern Minnesota. But I don't know why I'm seeing them.

I feel around at the shore. There's a kind of overhang here, made of mossy rocks. Underneath, empty space. I can't find the back of it with my hands, so I reach in with my feet and kick my legs around. Nothing.

In the city pool, I used to wear goggles. I wish I had them on now. Or I wish I could just sit over in the shallow end and splash my stars and jokes all day long. That would be fine with me.

But they are down there somewhere, father and son.

Dunk!

I swim beneath the overhang, opening my eyes onto murky green. Slamming them shut. My fingers finally touch a wall and feel their way up and up, till I break back through the surface. I spout like a porpoise, then float here for a while. My breathing echoes. "Hello?" That echoes, too. Pitch dark. Bobbing. Heavy earth smell.

My fingers find a muddy opening across the top.

No choice now. I pull myself up through. Like climbing through my bedroom window.

Tumble to a soft landing. Figure out how to sit up straight.

The first surprising thing is that it's not pitch dark. I can look around. It's green like the water, but not murky. Hundreds of little mushrooms glowing all over the wall. Sticking out like minty ears.

So...bioluminescence is the production and emission of light by a living organism, a process that occurs widely in marine vertebrates and invertebrates, such as jellyfish, as well as in insects, such as fireflies and glow worms, and in many varieties of fungus.

It's not cold in here. That's the second surprising thing. But the warmth comes along with that powerful smell again, cat litter and rotten eggs. My eyes sting and I have to breathe through my mouth. I pat what's beneath me and it's dried grass, so that's not the smell. Unless maybe they pee in here. I need to pee.

I force my pupils wide.

I try to, but they only grow at their own speed.

Little by little, I can tell the room is definitely not empty.

They sit perfectly still in three different spots. I can tell the shapes of the father and the wild boy, outlined by mushroom glow. The father is over to my right, maybe twenty feet away. This room must have a high ceiling. The wild boy's to my left. The third one sits in between. Between them in size, too.

"Sorry, should I leave?"

I can hear them all breathing. Like they have suddenly relaxed. They breathe through their noses and me, still my mouth. The wild boy scratches his shoulder. Sounds like the steel brush I've used on the goats.

"How long have you been living here?" I say this toward the father. Bowing my head low.

Nothing. Two minutes go by. The father stirs and takes a deep breath, then there's a replay from my dream: all the extinct animals going by.

"So why did you come to me now and not before?"

Hey listen to *me*! I...am...asking...someone...questions. I'm having a *conversation*.

I see a picture of *myself* lying curled on the yard. It was the night of the sleeping poison. I remember I tried to make it back to my room from the goat-house. I stumbled. My bedroom window looked a hundred miles away. I started crawling toward it. I thought I had made it back before Great White took me away and I woke up on the airplane. But I guess I only made it halfway across the yard.

The wild boy starts using two rocks for a steady *tap tap tap tap tap tap*.

Should I clap to match his rhythm? But I'm having too much fun in my *conversation*. I feel like I'm talking in my real voice.

"Is this place a...a cave?"

The middle shape thumps a quick foot onto the floor and the wild boy stops clacking.

Clear as day, in my mind, I see a hairy hand holding a mound of dirt.

"You...this *whole room*?"

I see tunnels leading to tunnels and rooms beneath rooms.

"But...how did you *dig* all of this out of solid *earth*?"

Again comes the slide show of animals, like a parade, and I understand.

"I understand!"

They have had plenty of time.

I'm sprawled in front of the TV at 11:45 PM with a half-empty bottle of whiskey in my lap.

"Well hey, Marlene, welcome to the show. All the way from northern Minnesota, is it?"

"That's right, Jimmy."

"So I guess you have planes up there now."

"Ha ha. Yes, we just got them in last week. Thanks for inviting me."

About an hour ago, when I caught the "Tonight Show" promo, I first reached for the whiskey and then considered calling Helen in from the goat-house. I think she's finally given up on trying to reach Marlene by phone. Our dedicated therapist has pulled out of our lives entirely.

Fallon says, "I understand you've been on quite a ride since...when was it?"

"That's right, Jimmy, this happened just *yesterday*."

A jolt of applause. "That's *sick*, Marlene. What an age we live in, huh? Nothing takes any time anymore."

"You said it."

"Props to our excellent producer, Erica, for snagging you first."

Far-flung portions of the crowd dutifully shout, "Thank you, Erica!"

Marlene reaches for Fallon's hand. How is she so damn poised? "Remember, though, you do have airplanes here."

Head cocked, he smirks at her gotcha. "Moving along.... Okay, so we've got your clip all set to go." A screen rises from the floor and stops midway between host and guest. "Can you walk us through what we're watching...from the beginning?"

"Sure thing. So as you can see here, I was standing well back from the others. That little girl sitting in the water there? I didn't agree with their approach, trying to capture her by force. You see, she is a profoundly autistic child and her home situation has become untenable. She's suffering from parental neglect and needs to be assessed in terms of—"

"Marlene, Marlene. We'll buy the textbook when it comes out!"

A swell of audience laughter.

"Right, I know. Ha! Sorry, Jimmy. I'm a little nervous. Well...okay, I was standing there documenting the event for my professional records when..."

As the Bigfoot shoots up from the middle of the pond, the audience gasps and Fallon grabs his head in panic, even though he's certainly seen the footage before, or why would he invite her on? He hops onto his desk and starts dancing like his feet are on fire. *Asshole ham. Hamhole.*

Meanwhile, the screen shows the ape swaying back and forth

and clearing water out of his eyes with his fingers.

The video pauses. Swig of whiskey. She addresses the crowd. "Now this next part you won't have seen online, because I saved it just for you folks."

Prick.

Fallon climbs back down. Someone in the control booth hits PLAY.

Dripping pond water, the monster's mouth hinges wide, and the mic on Marlene's smartphone is overwhelmed by the volume—you can hear distortion. But still, what comes out of my little television speakers is not a bad approximation of the real thing. And the sound that fills the New York studio itself must be downright dangerous. While the camera pans around, the roar is played twice more and people in their seats display priceless reactions. You'd think they were witnessing the Hindenburg disaster in person…and that their children were on board.

After a lengthy commercial break, everyone has finally simmered back down.

"Marlene, what about the *girl*? I assume she was rescued."

"No, not yet." The audience moans.

Idiotically, Fallon's taking for granted the very existence of Bigfoot—now suddenly demonstrated to the world…in my ravine—and focusing instead on the side issue.

Pam has obviously found a way to live *with* them and she's not in danger. If anything, the clueless oaf was protecting her from *me*. I explained this all to Helen yesterday, but she was unable to process it very well.

"Listen, this is an unprecedented situation and we need to figure out the best way forward."

"Where did this happen?"

"We are not releasing the location, for everyone's safety."

Yeah… "we."

"I mean, can you imagine a thousand hunters coming in there, all wanting to shoot and kill the specimen?"

"But you've told the authorities."

Marlene pauses. Fallon gapes his mouth in exaggerated disbelief, mugging for the camera.

"You have to understand," she hastens to explain, "it's a very delicate situation, how to approach a profoundly autistic child. If we go after her *directly*, she is likely to resist, which might only push her back toward this...this creature. Autism is a condition distinguished by an inability to—"

"And...we're back to the textbook!"

Helpless, hysterical laughter all around—from the crowd, from Fallon, from sidekick Steve Higgins...even from Marlene herself. Never has comic relief been more appreciated.

Seven hours later, I wake on the floor beside the empty bottle, hung over and battling hideous sunshine attacking me via three separate windows.

After brushing my teeth and making coffee, I sit at the computer to check out the brave new world. And sure enough, oh dear golly, it's everywhere. I can't find a single news feed that's not leading with the story—BIGFOOT FINALLY DISCOVERED!; WE ARE NOT ALONE!; HEEEERE'S SQUATCHY! Most of the articles feature a vivid screen capture of the roaring face. I see that Marlene has now posted the entire video, and it's been reposted all the way across the third planet from the sun. Funny to see a Turkish news feed with Pam's hefty associate looming behind the shouting anchorman.

Also on YouTube, though, my own video is nowhere to be found. In my drunken state, did I delete it out of spite? What's this? "Minnesota Bigfoot Hoax!!!" is gone, too. In fact, *all* the responses to my footage have been taken down. And to top it off, even my Victory123 channel itself has vanished.

I register a new account—Victory456—and am right in the middle of re-uploading my file—thinking, *This is good...after last night, it'll be taken seriously*—when I notice that my keyboard isn't working right, not responding to my fingers. And the cursor is moving around by itself. Some virus has hijacked my computer now? Pretty soon, the screen switches to a rapid scroll of files.

I check my smartphone—same story. In fact, here the screen is just plain blank.

So it's not a computer virus.

The front door swings open and I suddenly wish I owned a gun. But it's only Helen, in from the goat-house. She pours her usual bowl of Rice Chex, just as though those tasty squares are landing in the same reality today as they did yesterday.

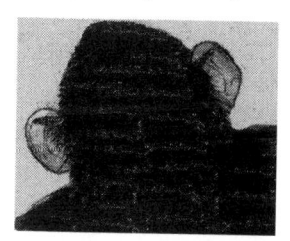

So...living underground has many advantages. Some animals, such as moles, live underground much or all of the time. It is their domain. Squirrel burrows include a deep nest chamber, in which the animal can sleep, rear its young, or simply hide from predators. Connected to this is an extensive network of tunnels with multiple entrances and exits.

What wakes me up is a strange kind of shrieking. Like someone being tickled. At first, I think it's my own voice till I touch my quiet mouth.

It's coming from across the room, where the middle-sized figure sits. Well, where she *used to* sit. I blink and learn the dim green lighting again. I can tell she's squatting now and reaching around with her arms, trying to catch something smaller that keeps ducking away. This way and that.

Suddenly, everything stops, except I'm laughing, filling up the room. The little one stands facing me. Its shape is just like the other three only its ears stick straight out. The face is dark but those ears catch the light from the mushrooms on the wall. This makes me laugh some more. The shapes are almost the same. These ears and those mushrooms!

Two circles startle me by lighting up red, the little one's eyes! And right away, the six other eyes in the room start glowing cool yellow. More bioluminescence. The little one turns its head. Looking around? Then, its eyes glow yellow, too. It crawls to sit in the middle one's lap, and then I can hear sounds of…nursing.

I picture the baby goat and the Mama, way back home.

I picture the Single Thing, still lying on its side up on the ridge.

The wild boy stands, turns, and disappears, but I can hear his footsteps. In a few seconds, I see his yellow eyes coming closer and closer. He's using a tunnel.

He hands some things to his father, then to the middle one.

His *mother*. Who I heard from the ridge, calling *Woooooooooooo!*

Now something lands and rolls at my feet. An apple!

The room fills with crunching. I join in. This is better than any discussion any group of people has ever had, back in the world.

The crunching gravel is not the UPS truck delivering my new gizmo but one of the white squad cars, delivering Sheriffs Fiske and DiMarco. They walk across the lawn with *very* strange expressions.

"We shouldn't be here," says DiMarco.

"Just thought we kind of…well, *owed* you," says Fiske, double-checking over his shoulders, even surreptitiously scanning the damn *sky*, "a quick heads-up."

"Huh?" I offer them seats on the porch, which they refuse, motioning back toward their car.

Fiske continues, "We told our supervisor what happened. He made some calls. He wouldn't have believed us, except there were, y'know..."

"Six of us," says DiMarco. "Two clammed up but they were so obviously shaken that it didn't matter. He got the picture."

"So anyway," says Fiske, "our supervisor, he was going to keep the matter in-house until, well..."

"Jimmy Fallon?" I suggest.

The sheriffs nod grimly.

"Then things really went south," says DiMarco, rolling her eyes.

"How so?" I ask.

They give me a few moments to think about it. My computer and phone are dead, but the TV still works, so this morning I've been watching events unfold—spontaneous demonstrations around the United States calling for the slaughter of these evil creatures; softer voices urging curiosity and calm study; frail Jane Goodall explaining in a BBC interview that "they are our cousins, not *monsters*."

Apparently, a whole lot of pent-up energy has just been waiting for convincing evidence to come along. CNN is already hyping this groundswell as **SASQUATCH FEVER!**

"Can't keep it contained?" I ask.

DiMarco lays a hand on my shoulder and gathers her thoughts. The sound of crunching gravel pre-empts whatever she was going to tell me.

Why are she and Fiske so afraid of a UPS truck? Because it's not a UPS truck.

I'll be warm again soon, back in the minty room. So it's easier to force myself out into the pond. The air up here is the freshest in history. I just tread water and breathe through my nose for a while. Remembering what a nose is for. Then, I travel to shallow water and pee.

On my way back to the deep water, just before I dip under, I hear the voices of men. Not again!

I can't see them yet.

I catch sight of my quilt on shore. In the leek field. Can't let them see that. Can't let them see that.

I picture myself dragging it under, then trying to wrestle it into the room, even though it will be filled with water and ten times heavier. And down there it would never dry out.

I swim over, climb the bank. Pull the quilt around my shoulders. Start running for the far valley wall. Partway up, I dive into a thick pocket of shade. Gasping for air.

The men last time were some kind of police. Now these men below me are *soldiers*. They surround the pond. All get down on one knee. To do this, most of them have to get their pants wet in the marsh. They all aim their guns where the father came up. The exact spot on the water. How do they know?

"Mr. James Manchester, at this particular point in time, you need to consider your home and property on lock-down ahead of possible seizure under the authority of the Eminent Domain Clause of the Fifth Amendment of the United States Constitution."

This has to be a joke. The military man in front of me wears an impressive uniform with shoulder stripes, and sure, he arrived in an olive-green Humvee driven by another soldier-type—*but still...*

"Diet Coke?" It's all I can think to say. I'm all alone. Fiske and DiMarco drove off immediately, and Helen is still in the kitchen, munching her Rice Chex, probably staring into space.

"Sir, I'm not certain you recognize the gravity of the situation."

"Well, of course I've *heard* of Eminent Domain, but doesn't that apply to government take-over of private land for...like... highways and pipelines, or that type of thing?"

"'In blighted or deteriorated areas that present a threat to public safety,'" he recites from memory, "'the government has the right to seize property through Eminent Domain.'"

"'Blighted or deteriorated'?" I gesture around at my unspoiled Eden.

"Sir!"

"'Public safety'?"

"Mr. Manchester," Commander Eminent Domain points out, "we attempted to inform you reasonably."

"If you're for real, you better *attempt* to replace my fucking computer."

Just then, five more olive-green Humvees come screaming single file down the driveway, covered with ingenious camouflage—painted leaves. They skid to halts in the yard, one clipping the goat-house and striking the nanny. I can hear her neck crack beneath the tire.

The commander turns toward his troops, issuing orders.

Soldiers exit their vehicles and fan out past the kiddie pool and the apple tree, some taking pictures, others stringing thick orange tape along the tree line.

Helen runs outside. "Jim, what's going on?!"

I can't find any words, no matter how close she gets, finally grabbing my arm when she spots the dead goat.

Working efficiently, the soldiers unload large duffel bags and backpacks, also olive green, piling them up against the fallen tree.

Helen and I stand mesmerized. Within minutes, an open-sided tent, maybe twenty by twenty, takes its place before us, stabilized by ropes staked into our lawn. Five bright red generators go under the tent. Two are switched on and connected by cords to laptops, external hard drives, and plasma screens.

Commander Eminent Domain strides back up to us. "Ma'am, be assured that we *will* recover your daughter safe and sound." He has to raise his voice over the generators. "That is PHASE ONE, Ma'am." Behind him, his men assemble assault rifles with intimidating metallic precision. "So you and Mr. Manchester would be best advised to remain inside the home. You'll be safe in there."

"I hope you treat our daughter a little better than that goat." Without following where my finger points, he squints at me.

"So...what's PHASE TWO?" Helen asks.

"I'm afraid that's classified. At this particular point in time, you need to let us do our job and there should be no problems. Your property is on lock-down."

He returns to his men, who are testing walky-talkys and synchronizing watches. Then, they hoist backpacks and gun straps over their shoulders, lift duffels, and deploy briskly into the forest.

Two soldiers remain to install a large satellite dish outside Pam's bedroom window, where they find the best angle into the sky.

taptaptaptaptaptap

The wild boy's crouching nearby on the valley wall. Inside another shadow higher up. Using his two stones very quietly. To get my attention. Once I see him, he stops tapping.

How did you get out here, Wild Boy?

But he won't even look at me.

Not through the pond.

I watch the soldiers. We'll keep an eye on them together. Inside my quilt, I flap my hands and rock back and forth.

One soldier shouts "Release!" Another tosses something into the air that curves down and splashes in the center of the pond.

The guns are steady.

Five seconds later...*BWOOOOSH!!!* A swell of gray water rises. Breaks apart. Falls back into place.

Everybody down there on one knee freezes for half a minute. Concentrating. Concentrating.

I picture the minty room. Flooded. The little one better be quiet down there. Be quiet!

Above me, the wild boy's eyes are shut and he's swaying back and forth. Just like me.

"All clear!" shouts the first soldier. "Stand down!"

In the wild leek field, two soldiers help a third soldier put on diving gear. A vest. Flippers. Face mask. Silver tanks. I tell myself you don't need a diving suit to get to the minty room. These soldiers don't know anything about the minty room. Or about our underground life.

Since I'm not permitted to sit on my own front porch, Helen and I hole up in Pam's room all afternoon, and I must say it's good to get to know her again. Turns out that when she's not feeling cornered and overwhelmed, she's a sincere and trusting soul. Unfortunately, in the present situation, with an occupying force outside the window, she's a bit *too* trusting.

"So you're saying you feel comfortable under siege like this?"

"We've already seen how powerless ordinary police are. Considering what we're up against, I'd rather have the military here, really taking care of things, retrieving her, than to have Pam out in that valley alone with...and no way for us to reach her."

"You really think that's what they're doing out there?"

"What *else* would they be doing?"

"Big-game hunting would be my hunch."

"Jim, they made us a *promise*."

"Why would they care about one little kid in the grand scheme of things?"

"Their—"

"I mean, they wiped my computer just to destroy that video clip, because they know it was real. And to send me an unmistakable message."

"Their whole mission is to protect the citizens of the United States from harm."

Almost forgot—Helen's a Republican.

We go round and round. I consider shattering her worldview by telling her about the thuggish Eminent Domain threat. Instead, I decide to share the "Kid Genius!" Facebook page.

Watching Pam's Kansas City performance nearly destroys the poor woman. In tears, she yanks open the window and pleads with the nearest uniform for an update.

"Ma'am," he says, "I can tell you we are making excellent progress on PHASE ONE."

"Oh, thank you, *thank* you."

At sunset, emotionally exhausted, we finally surrender to the blessed distraction of television.

Sasquatch Fever is taking many forms. Christians are proclaiming the End of Days, the return of the Nephilim—demonic giants from the Bible. Reports are surfacing of rural residents packing up and fleeing to the cities because they recognize "that pond" as the one near them, not believing Marlene's that it's in Minnesota. No fewer than eighteen US lawmakers are calling for congressional hearings into the implications for public welfare. Environmental organizations are demanding that vast new regions be set aside as protected habitat—pointing out that hundreds of verified sightings have occurred in every state except Hawaii—while furious representatives of the timber and natural gas industries denounce this "rush to judgment." And breaking news out of Indiana—the shooting death of a man who was part of a vigilante hunting group; said the ring-leader, "We was just trying to bag the one his grandmother seen."

Right in the middle of an interview with a California woman whose young son disappeared years ago from their back yard, leaving nothing for authorities to discover but massive, five-toed footprints, Don Lemon touches his earpiece. "Excuse me.... Okay, I'm just getting word that the President is ready to make a statement. We take you now to the Press Briefing Room."

President Clinton stands at the podium in front of a large, drop-down screen displaying a still image of the pond—*our* pond. Helen and I look at each other. Why replay the video?

"My fellow Americans," she begins, "these past several days have seen a sudden rise in irrational thinking in our country. I might even call it *magical* thinking, with many people jumping to wild conclusions. I think you all know what I'm referring to. I'm here tonight to put your minds to rest. What I'm going to show you now is a different piece of video footage but shot at the very same location."

Hillary steps aside and I can see that, sure enough, we and the sheriffs are nowhere to be seen, though the camera angle matches Marlene's—nor is Pam's little head.

And yet, here comes the ape man again, surging upward to his midsection, water pouring off his head and shoulders. Or no....

It takes maybe five seconds for me to see through the sham. The color is actually on target, the hair's about the right length, shoulders good 'n' broad, head the same general shape, too, and face even bearing some vague resemblance. But the arms are all wrong, way too short.

"Oh my God," Helen laughs, "that's totally *fake*!"

When the figure opens his mouth, the roar does sound perfect...because they've dubbed in the original audio!

What happens next has us literally gasping for breath on the couch. The guy reaches up and removes his Bigfoot head, revealing his own much tinier one and his mischievous, grinning face. Holding the head under one arm, he waves to the camera with the other. And then, he heaves away the head—*splash!* Popping up next to him is a frogman whose shoulders he's been standing on. He takes off his mask and now they're both waving and cracking up. And...scene.

At the podium, looking smug, President Clinton nods and settles the press corps back down with a knowing hand. "So you see just how quickly a shameless hoax like this can lead to civil unrest and could even have potentially threatened the very fabric of our society, if we hadn't managed to uncover this second video clip so quickly.

"In future, ladies and gentlemen, can we try to be a lot more thoughtful? Beware of agitators who would prey upon our gullibility and exploit our collective desire for excitement. Apply common sense, people: If such a thing as"—chuckle—"Bigfoot were even remotely possible, don't you think we'd all know about it by now? As a matter of fact, we'd have *welcomed* them a long time ago as fellow creatures on this earth to be respected and understood...indeed, to be *learned* from. And public safety would be my administration's paramount concern.

"These clowns," she continues, gesturing back toward the blank screen, "they probably hold no malice in their hearts. Homeland Security is interrogating them as we speak, just to make sure, and we also want to talk to Marlene S., whose real name is Marlene Stevens, from St. Cloud, Minnesota." A freeze frame from the "Tonight Show" fills the screen behind the President. "If anyone has information on this woman's whereabouts, please contact your local law enforcement."

"Ohhhh," Helen whispers, "she's in *trouble*."

"I ask you to imagine for a moment the dark designs that *terrorists* could attempt to unleash upon our nation after destabilizing and distracting us with such a trick in the future. That's why it is vital, it is *imperative* that we all keep our eye on the ball.

"In closing, my friends, rest assured that if anything like Bigfoot or aliens one day turns out to be real, believe me"—broad wink—"I'll letcha know. You'll hear it here first. But for now, we can all breathe a sigh of relief, chalk it up to experience, and return to our familiar lives. Hey, they might not be quite as dramatic as they seemed ten minutes ago, but God bless our ordinary little lives, our liberty...and God bless the United States of America."

Frantically shouted questions are ignored as she briskly exits the room—"How was this second video found?"; "What about the physical evidence for Bigfoot?"; "The Melba Ketchum DNA results, why are they being suppressed?"; "Madame President, where does the *child* fit into the picture?"

Outside on the lawn, fifty or sixty soldiers erupt into cheers and applause. A man's voice rises. "They're *interrogating* us, Chipper!"

"Yeah, hope we don't crack under the pressure!" Peals of laughter.

I pace the living room, telling Helen, "That's it. This is fucking nuts. No Internet, no cell service, but there's still good old 'information' and good old landline. I'm calling in the media, every outlet I can think of, starting with FOX 9 News."

She solemnly hands me the telephone.

"Break this thing wide open. We don't live in some kind of totalitarian—"

The line is dead.

We're underground again. It's another room. Different shape. Two rough corners this time. We're inside the valley wall. Same dried-grass floor. Same four of us sitting in different spots. Same not breathing through my nose.

The little one is playing around in one corner. I can see her better now. There's more light in this room. Not from mushrooms. From small holes in the ceiling. Letting sun through. One ray shows a heap of bones in another corner. With flies.

This room is more like a cave. The walls have some dirt and some sharp rocks jutting out. And there's one wall that's smooth stone. When I first got here, I laid my hands on there. And my face.

After the explosion at the pond, the soldiers pretended to be the father. Some kind of joke. It *must* have been a joke because they all laughed so much. I didn't get it. The wild boy didn't get it, either. Trying to tell the father they were going to pull his head off? Is that funny?

I like jokes. Maybe it's the kind of joke that only normal people understand.

It's almost Halloween. Maybe it was a Halloween costume.

I can't see the little one's face. I'll bet she's a girl. About as tall as I am but acts like a toddler. She's squeaking and chirping. Doing flips. Trying to make her mother laugh. I can't see the mother's face, either. She has big breasts filled with milk. I lick my lips.

Instead of laughing, she just keeps trying to grab the girl out of the air when she flips by. One time, she catches her. Tickles her. The girl...I *think* it's a girl...wriggles out and hits the ground hard. She pretends to be hurt. When the mother leans over, she springs up and runs away. Hilarious. So hilarious!

She tumbles into a ray of sunlight. She *is* a girl!

All the rest of us, nobody's looking at anybody else. Or talking. This is very, very relaxing.

It's not cold in this room, either, but wrapping myself in the quilt just feels wonderful. I guess I could ask more questions. Maybe get some new, interesting pictures. But I'm too happy just breathing with this family. And I don't wonder anything right now.

The smell is even worse. Not me and the wild boy, but the others got soaked by the flood down in the minty room. From the explosion.

I don't get that part of the joke.

The little girl's jokes. Those I get. She cracks me up. I should call her Funnybone! I jab my elbow on my hip. The *twang* tells me I've picked the right name. Finally a name in here.

After they played their joke, the soldiers went away. Marching back out of the valley.

Then, the wild boy showed me the way in. Up here on the valley wall. Maybe he wasn't showing me. Maybe he just lifted the rock out of its hole and climbed down inside. Like a cork in a bottle.

What a huge rock for him to lift!

I didn't follow the first time. I didn't know if I was supposed to.

Minutes later, his head popped back. He scanned the whole valley. Taking pictures, I'm pretty sure. Then he climbed out and went to stand by a tree. He still wouldn't look at me. Just swayed and swayed and double-checked the different parts of the valley.

He went back into the hole. I went in, too, quilt and all.

Funnybone is nursing again. I don't try to go closer to anybody else. I can tell they don't want me to. And I don't want to. I've got my own spot. Everything is free and steady in here with them. There is no pressure. I have never felt this way with people back in the world. I can press my eyes and flap my hands. They can each do what they want to do at their own speed.

The wild boy likes to click his stones together. The father likes to sway slowly from side to side. He likes to hum in his throat. Notes like the low end of a harmonica. When the mother gets tired of reaching for her little girl, she just leans back against the dirt wall and nods her head. Not nodding *yes*. Just calming herself down.

Funnybone is the only one who looks at me, but not for long. Quick glances in between tumbling routines. Every time she does, I can't help giggling. I don't use my speaking voice. Most of the time, I forget I even have one. But I really crack up when she starts copying my hand-flapping and head-slapping! We do it back and forth a few times before the mother thumps her foot.

Funnybone stops playing. Crawls back into her mother's lap. Listen to her swallowing that milk.

This is going to be a good life for us.

Gulping it down.

What the hell?

People in war zones tend to sleep lightly...

At 3:12, I hear the distant breaking of glass and lie frozen until the basement door unlatches and swings open. I never lock that door. There's no way into the basement except a little window at ground level. You'd really have to mess yourself up to—

Oh, Crap.

I find Marlene standing in the kitchen, trembling, face covered in blood. Instinctively, I take her in my arms, like an excellent human being. Okay, an awkward one. "You're safe now, you're safe now. What *happened*?"

She fights free and walks in circles, far too hysterical to sit. Hyperventilating. I wish I hadn't finished off that whiskey. I pull her some paper towels, especially for the gash on her forehead. She keeps looking out the windows, where the regiment has set up a row of sleeping tents. A few are still on watch, smoking cigarettes beside a campfire.

I douse all the lights except the dim one over the stove.

After a while, Marlene recovers herself somewhat, thanks to Helen's emerging from Pam's bedroom and administering a far more therapeutic hug.

"I didn't think it would happen so *fast*," she whispers, circling again, swabbing blood. At least she has her wits about her enough to keep her voice down. "When Hillary outed me, I knew I might have to be careful, maybe even leave St. Cloud for a while, but when I got back from the airport tonight, a *crowd* had already formed outside my house. I couldn't believe how angry they were. I tried to dialogue with them..."

You mean "talk"?

"...but they were chanting things like 'Terrorist! Terrorist!' and 'Attention Whore! Attention Whore! Attention Whore!'"

Marlene cries.

"They hurt you," says Helen, wetting the paper towel and dabbing it on individual cuts.

"No, this is from your basement window. But they would have. I barely got out of there. A couple of them had baseball bats."

Rinsing the paper towel in the sink, Helen shakes her head. "Anyone can tell that new video is a cheap imitation."

"Nobody wants to believe that, so they won't," Marlene answers flatly. "Perception is reality."

I want to know, "Why did you come here, of all places?"

"I could have gone to any number of friends' houses, but I didn't want to put them in danger."

"Oh, thanks!" My laugh comes out dry and empty.

"I came here because nobody knows where it is."

"Nobody besides the United States Government," I remind her.

"I just mean, they're not likely to connect me with it, since I haven't officially worked with your family in years. Obviously, I knew some of those at the pond today would probably still be hanging around. I parked down the road and snuck up here, just in case."

Finally, she sits, head in hands. "I never expected *this* level of presence."

"It's a belly-of-the-beast type of situation," I point out helpfully.

"By the time I saw them all, it was too late. I'd committed. I hid behind the house. I've got no place else to go."

"And at least they're not an angry mob," says Helen.

"And let's not forget, they're sworn to serve and protect."

She shoots me a look.

An hour later, we start to hear a commotion on the lawn. Soldiers stirring awake, coughing. Tent poles clinking together. Machinery being handled. Humvees roaring to life, their headlights ruining the night. Commander Eminent Domain barking orders.

We all jump at his sharp knocks, Marlene retreating to the darkest corner of the room.

"We're moving out," he says when I open the door.

"Under cover of night," I say. "Good thinking."

"Wait, wait, wait, wait, no *wait*." Helen hops from foot to foot. "What about Pamela? You *promised* you'd recover her."

"Ma'am, we were unable to locate your daughter. On behalf of the United States Government, I do apolog—"

"You didn't even look." She sags, utterly defeated. "You just made a bad video."

I hear her trudging back down the hall toward Pam's bedroom.

"When will we see you again?" I ask him.

"That's up to you, Mr. Manchester. Remember what we talked about at the beginning. I'd hate to have to go ahead and make it stick."

"Mm."

"You're going to want to live a quiet life from now on." He squints. "A *smarter* life. So we don't have to proceed to PHASE TWO. No more sharing your fuzzy neighbors with the world, understood? Better yet, just leave them alone. Neither side of this thing is anywhere near ready for the other. Think of us"—he gestures behind him—"as peacekeeping troops."

"Guardians."

"Absolutely!"

I actually salute and he actually smiles. We are super-close friends now.

"Here's your compensation for the livestock." He hands me a crisp five-hundred-dollar bill. "Oh, and by the way," he adds, directing his voice to Marlene's corner, "we know exactly who you are, Lady, and you can relax—Madam President already took care of you."

One week later, it's almost as though the military was never here. As soon as they left, the phone worked again, and my computer sprang back to life—*presto*—minus my precious footage, of course. They turfed the fire pit back over, reeled in the thick orange tape, folded and packed the satellite dish at Pam's window, smoothed the tent-pole divots, and even hauled away the dead nanny goat. Helen bottle-feeds her baby with formula from our local farm and yard store.

Things have settled into a strangely predictable routine around here. Helen has told her understanding family that she can't return home until this situation is resolved. *Good old Clifford. Good old Tucker.*

Marlene, of course, is sticking around, too. I find I like her better now that she's a national disgrace—it takes a person down a few pegs. She even takes turns with the bottle-feeding.

By far the majority of our time is spent watching Pam.

Here's how it happened.

After the special-ops Bigfoot team thoughtfully cleared the way so that the UPS truck could deliver my Next-Generation Nano Hummingbird, it took me a whole long day just to get comfortable operating the tiny drone. It's a lot harder than the first one—joy stick much more sensitive, the bird capable of precision adjustments in flight.

Luckily, it's equipped with object-avoidance sensors, or else I'd be slamming into trees.

I learned how to maneuver through the forest pretty well, and then came the tedious hours of surveillance. Pam was just nowhere to be found. I was wishing I could afford a flock of drones and a team of pilots. After hardly setting foot in the woods during my entire life here, I became an expert on every wrinkle of topography within a one-mile radius.

And then—time stamp 2:32 PM, four days ago—it finally happened.

What a moment. I called Helen into the room and, side by side on the couch, we feasted on the console screen.

Out past the ravine on the far side, there's an open plateau. I must have checked it fifty times already that same day—it was part of my regular surveillance route. Now I was back, hovering at a hundred feet, when she simply emerged from the tree line, pretty as you please.

Determined not to startle her, I peeled off and descended into a dark grove, then made my way tree by tree back toward the clearing. When she noticed me, she lit up.

"Hello!" she said, waving. "You're *green*."

The first-generation Nanos were still kind of noisy, but this new model is virtually silent, which allows for a microphone in addition to a video camera.

"Her eyes..." said Helen. "I used to look into them like this for hours when she was little." And thank God the audio doesn't go both ways because then she burst out sobbing—the sound of pure relief.

After that, I danced around Pam as she tried to catch me. Truthfully, it was all I could do not to fly *toward* her hands. Helen and I both gasped when I brought the bird to a mid-air stand-still just two or three feet away and our daughter gazed into our eyes. I hadn't felt so close to her in years, or so close to this woman sitting beside me. Not since our wedding day, in fact. If not for Marlene in the room with us, I might have tried something.

"Look, she's made an outfit from her quilt...a halter-top." And bunchy shorts. It's gotten pretty chilly these days—leaves are falling—so I'm happy she's no longer running around naked up there. "And, Jim, *slippers* out of rhubarb leaves. Maybe she'd like one of those rhubarb pies I used to make?"

Now, every day, all three of us wake up, eat breakfast, and then proceed to revel in the "Pamela Manchester Show." She's even worked *us* into *her* routine, meeting the bird in the field at the start of each day. And she's seldom alone, either, so it's more like "Pamela Manchester and Friends."

Most of the time, she's with a bushy, coal-colored young one with a round face, big ears, and pointy head, who is about her height but three times less scrawny. And full of energy. The two will play a version of tag together without ever touching. Or sometimes, they will play long-distance patty-cake where they sit maybe thirty feet apart and mimic each other's hand movements—flapping, clapping, slapping their heads, wiggling fingers, etc.

"If I didn't know better," Marlene mused when she first saw

this, sliding on her glasses, "I'd say that female juvenile primate is on the autism spectrum, too. Ha! Remarkable. Professor Grandin would love this."

"*Temple* Grandin?" Helen asked.

"Yes, I did my graduate work with her at Colorado State."

Today, Marlene points at the screen. "Notice how they're not facing each other and never look at each other...or don't *seem* to." She's constantly commentating, which is getting on our nerves. "This is called 'parallel play.' Secretly, they are fully aware of one another, as you can plainly tell by their 'mirroring' behavior. This is typical behavior for autistic children to engage in."

"And...we're back to the textbook." I regret saying it instantly but she takes it in stride, absorbed by her new case study. And anyway, we watched Jimmy Fallon issue a public apology for "aiding and abetting a fraud"—he looked so pathetic, so *personally* wounded, that we eventually had to laugh.

It's late afternoon, and I've got to head home. I've lost track of our daughter, plus my battery is running low. I wish I could land this thing on a branch and just keep recording all day, but I only get two hours and fifteen minutes of flight time before I need to recharge.

I take one more swoop into the ravine and there she sits at the bottom, drinking from the brook, splashing it in front of her face. She waves when she sees me, as always, but I can't linger, terrified I'll fall dead on the bank and she'll discover the camera lens—the size of a pencil eraser.

Buzzing swiftly up the bank, I fly past two males who are spying on her, each crouching behind a tree.

Once I land safely on the lawn, I go back and replay that clip in slow motion. I can tell exactly where their eyes are aimed. I'm kind of glad their midsections are out of frame—*perverts*.

Judging from their lanky physiques, I'd say those two spies are much bigger than Pam's young playmate, but much smaller than King Kong from the pond.

Whenever any of the Bigfoot have appeared on screen, I've hit RECORD. All of this video, maybe ten hours, is stored on my DVR, but that's the end of the line. I can never post a scrap of it on the Internet, of course, or even work with the footage on my computer—"Sasquatch Fever" was destined to be a twenty-four-hour bug.

I know the little bird isn't real. Well, it's real, but it's a machine.

I thought it was a hummingbird for a minute till I realized there are no nectar flowers up here anymore. They all turned brown and fell off. Hummingbirds migrate south by this time of year.

But I was glad. I always missed the helicopter that crashed on the ridge. This one doesn't crash. This one plays with me every morning. I love it. Sometimes, it zips over to Funnybone for a while and watches her flap her hands and smack her head. She learned that from me! I tried to teach her the funny bone trick, but she's got way too much muscle and hair piled on top of her hip bones.

From her, I've learned to do flips. I couldn't do these wrapped in a quilt, so I had to rip it up into clothes. When I play chase with her, she's on all fours. It's natural for her. Like a horse. I run on all fours, too. I've done this ever since I can remember, so it's pretty natural for me, too. She's way faster. Even when I get up on two feet, I'm a slow poke. And also, she zigzags. No fair!

I bet even her brother couldn't catch her, if he wanted to try. If he didn't always ignore her.

I'm cold sometimes. The leaves are falling. But I'm not worried about winter anymore, because underground I'm never cold. Dried grass is my new quilt and the room fills up with body heat. I'll bet the father could heat my old house all by himself. In the high room, I lay my hands and my cheeks on the cool stone wall sometimes.

I breathe through my nose in there. Don't even notice the smell anymore.

I used to wonder how my wildness was going. Not now. They're really not very wild like I used to think of this word. I used to think it meant prowling around snarling and furious. Making enemies. Ready to tear animals apart all the time. Animals and even people.

But life with this family is calm and organized. Even when we come up onto the ground in the daytime. We mostly sit around. Eating leaves. Digging for roots that are good for chewing. Swaying and clacking stones. Drumming on the ground with our hands and feet. Building things with sticks.

I learned my lesson when I tried to change things. I got jealous watching Funnybone drink from her mother. Trying to crawl close was a big, big mistake. That's when she *did* turn wild against me. For about five seconds.

Distance is my lesson.

Up in the woods, we take cat naps, but never all at the same time. Usually, it's the father who stays awake, leaning against his favorite thick tree. Listening for trouble.

But trouble never comes. Not since the soldiers. When the little bird first showed up, acting so strange, the father made us escape. We all ran fast with twists and turns till we lost it. Then, we went underground for a while. But now, he just ignores it or swats it away if it gets too close.

Airplanes fly overhead. Far-away cars use the road. No big deal. I smile to myself because I never have to ride in those two machines again.

Once, Great White's voice. Like a quick mayfly past my ear. I can't hear his words. He says something and then laughs. I know he is on the lawn because I also hear a car door slam. My wind is just right. I hear *mehhhhhh!* I picture my bed, my blue pool, my piggy bank, my hairbrush, my wild animal posters, and everything else down there, one by one. And then, Great White laughs again and is gone.

What we enjoy doing are very few things. We enjoy them over and over. The shape of our days is like the same piece of sculpture. We hardly ever talk. They don't understand me when I try. Instead, we sit here thinking in pictures. Sometimes by ourselves, sometimes sharing. It is never boring. That's how we talk. We just pass the time together. And the best part? When we're all sitting together, I never have to look anyone in the face.

The days are long. If I miss my Kindle and all those games, I just reboot my brain. Start laughing at Funnybone or make t-pees or watch my ant colonies. Or whatever. The hours fall away by themselves. They know how to.

Well, one thing is different. The wild boy is starting to bother me. Mostly when his friend is around. His friend is a boy with sandy hair. I call him Sandy. He's from a different family. Together, they try to boss me around. Not with their voices or their hands. They won't try to touch me because the father is never far away. He makes the rules and nobody wonders what they are.

They try to boss me with sound waves. Not hard enough to make me sick like that policeman in the valley. Just hard enough to make me nervous. And they look at my body. That's another reason I made the quilt into clothes. So I wouldn't have to keep holding it around me.

I used to love looking at the wild boy. Taking pictures of him. It used to make me feel weak and happy. But this was back when he wouldn't look at me. Sandy ruined all that space. Now they stare at me.

First, they wrestle. They shoot each other with sound waves and try to pretend it doesn't hurt. And this gets them into a mood.

They turn toward me. They hit me with waves, too. This makes me feel weak. Not in the good way.

That's when I go find Funnybone, and we play some more.

I keep asking myself, *If they are apes, why don't they just jump her?* I'm extremely glad they don't. I'd have to go up there, and I don't even own a gun.

Those two lanky adolescents especially. Frick and Frack. They show such restraint, but that could end any second. Should I move out of these hobby drones? I bet there's a black market for military surplus models armed with hellfire missiles.

Then again, our once-bottomless "Kid Genius!" oil well has finally bled dry. We've been missing gigs, breaking contracts left and right. Toxic Facebook messages threaten lawsuits. Discussion threads are boiling over.

But nobody dared to use the H-word until FOX 9 News, who joined the mob this morning, telling the world how I weaseled out of the live remote spot—"Pamela Manchester is the real victim here, a special-needs puppet controlled by an exploiting father. This whole thing is a HOAX! Maybe James Manchester can pull the wool over the eyes of an audience in a carefully monitored situation, but he's terrified to subject his scam to the bright glare of our cameras!"

The news station goes on to announce that they are planning to produce an exposé of our case unless I come forward with an immediate explanation.

Others jump on the bandwagon all day long—"No WONDER they never showed up at our conference. His daughter probably broke free of his influence, leaving him in the lurch"; "We should have known it was too good to be true"; "That ink and paper illusion, what a pile of garbage! Girl obviously couldn't memorize twenty different thumbprints so fast. That last guy was an inside job!"

Roger Rosenberg himself, whose print Pam identified by name in Kansas City, weighs in, swearing he had no behind-the-scenes knowledge and had never met us before. Yet, even good old Roger tosses a small grenade—"I don't like feeling that I may have been set up."

What, *me* worry? I'm far too busy in front of the other screen.

Right at the moment, Frick and Frack are crouched together in a tree above Pam and the juvenile girl. The girl is so full of energy! She scampers up the tree and swats them on their butts. Even though they see her coming, they can't do a thing about it. She is unbelievably quick, zipping on all fours like some turbocharged black bear. And when she does this to the boys, they suddenly transform from shady peeping toms into harmless, pesky older brothers.

Helen sits beside me, rejoicing equally in Pam's survival, social acceptance, and obvious good cheer. Occasionally, she fills me in on further examples of feral children who thrived in the wild. "'Samantha of Borneo'"—air quotes—"lived with a troupe of proboscis monkeys for nine years, subsisting on fruits and tubers until the end of British colonial rule in 1963, when her family recovered her and brought her back to England. Five months later, she 'died of a broken heart.'"

Marlene, for her part, is evidently planning revenge against the United States Government and a dramatic professional make-over as the Jane Goodall of Bigfoot. I thought that was going to be my daughter's role, but she's a little bit too involved.

Our therapist takes copious notes on her iPad and dutifully sends them along to her mentor, Temple Grandin, world-famous autistic author and crusader for the humane treatment of animals. Unfortunately, however, Temple Grandin, world-famous autistic author and crusader for the humane treatment of animals, doesn't seem to care. Whenever I ask if she's heard back from her, Marlene deflects the question with fresh observations.

"Notice how the young males in the tree here continue to employ anti-social behavior. Instead of interacting with one another, they are self-stimulating."

"They *better* not be!"

"No, Jim, in this context there is no sexual connotation. It's the equivalent of Pamela's hand-flapping: repetitive behavior that soothes the autistic child."

"I know, I know, Marlene. *Joking*."

"See how he's patting his palm against the tree trunk there? The exact same way every time. Meanwhile, the other one is clicking his teeth together. When you approach him..."—okay, I'll take the bait...I hover the bird in close—"see, you can make out his jaw twitching again and again. But even when you recede again and focus on the others...listen carefully...you can still hear the clicking in the background. I've been monitoring it continually for the past seventy-nine minutes. These two are filled with nervous energy and unable to relax. I'd love to get in there and *work* with these subjects using Applied Behavioral Analysis." She nibbles the stem of her glasses. "I'd probably go with the Rapid Prompting Method. Would you like me to explain?"

"Nope."

Helen says, "Yes, please."

"Well, it relies on positive reinforcement in order to teach new skills, increase on-task behavior, and promote social interaction. We often find that..."

It happens just after noon. We don't catch the beginning—whatever sparks it—but the sounds alert me to joy-stick over in that direction. Angry, guttural words are being shouted back and forth.

Apes don't talk.

When I finally get the action in frame, we can see it's Frick and Frack. Their words have turned into raw growls and they're squaring off under a maple tree. It's windy and red and yellow leaves fall around them. Now they lock arms like sumo wrestlers. But *unlike* sumo wrestlers, they are trying to bite each other's shoulders—epic canine teeth exposed.

I glance at Marlene. "You wanted interaction."

She's glued to the screen, shushing me.

Helen says, "Where's Pam!?"

I didn't do anything. I was just sitting here munching on wild leeks. Then, I cleared away colorful leaves and started drawing a woolly mammoth with a stick in the dirt. Lying down on one elbow. Sticking out my tongue sideways to concentrate.

A foot lands next to my drawing and I look up and up. It's not the wild boy. It is Sandy. Looking down at me. Not at my face but at my legs and belly. I sit up straight and stare at one blond knee.

Nothing happens. Sandy breathes.

Where is the father?

Then, everything happens too fast.

The wild boy appears from somewhere and starts yelling at Sandy. Strange words. Then, they blast each other with sound waves. They start wrestling. This time it is not a game.

It's a terrible fight. I can't even watch. I cover my ears and run to find Funnybone. She and her mother and father must be down in the high room. Why isn't he up here keeping an eye on us? I thought he was perfect.

Should I go get him? How do you go get a giant?

I try sending him pictures. Pictures of the fight. I sit by my half-drawing and rock back and forth. Sending pictures. Slapping my head and humming as loud as I can.

How much time goes by?

Next thing, Sandy is gone and there is blood all over the colorful leaves. The wild boy is catching his breath. Hands on his knees. Blood drips from his shoulders.

The rest of the family is finally here. The father is looking in the direction of the other family. They live across the field. Down in the next valley. The mother keeps trying to touch her son's wounds. He keeps turning his back to her.

Funnybone tries to sit down by his feet. He kicks her away every time.

We all hold our heads so they won't explode from what we've just witnessed.

On the screen, it's finally over. Pam and the victorious boy sit back to back. Well, not quite. There is space between them.

I monitor them through bare branches, keeping a respectful distance—Marlene has recommended less "helicopter parenting."

The father must be punishing Sandy? Sandy's father? The whole family?

We're in the high room. The mother licks the wounds. I can hear her every time I wake up. Sometimes the wild boy is whining. "He's just a kid," I whisper to myself.

Funnybone whimpers, too. In her corner.

The father comes home. I hear a load of something drop on the floor. Not a dead body. Something light. Plants? The mother chews them and spits them out. Chews and spits. Chews and spits.

Sun rays come through again. We are waking up. The wild boy has dried green paste on his shoulders. Pressed deep into his chestnut hair. Lines of it on the gray skin of his face, too. There are healing leaves still on the floor.

The wild boy and I sit by the climbing tree. Watching the leaves fall around us. When I scooch closer, he lets me. He lets me lean against him this time. Right against his back.

Like a wall.

He is letting me! I can't believe this. How long till he pulls away?

I pay all kinds of attention to an orange leaf in my hand. Tilting it in the sunlight.

And then, he tells me his name. Not with his voice. He just drops it into my head like a penny into my piggy bank: Rantea-Took.

Now *that* wasn't so hard, was it?

I look around. My wind goes in a slow swirl around us. Around me and Rantea-Took. Me and Rantea-Took.

The sun is climbing.

The little green bird is late today.

"*When*, Marlene?" I don't have to ask her *what* she did. And from the look on her face, I sure don't have to wonder whether I'm accusing the wrong person.

"Excuse me?"

We're standing face to face, weary but alarmed. The hummingbird lies idle on the kitchen table beside the butter dish. Outside the window, a cargo helicopter the size of my house has just landed on the lawn.

"I know what you did, asshole!" I pound the table. "You videoed my screen with your tablet and sent the footage to Temple Grandin."

Marlene flinches. "Jim, listen, listen. It was the only way to get her atten—"

"And put us all at risk in the process? Including Pam? *When*?!"

"You were in the bathroom and Helen went to the store."

I remember. There's an auto pilot switch so the drone just hovers in place when I have to leave the controls for a minute.

Marlene dumps herself into a chair, reaches across the table for Helen's hand. The hand is unwilling.

"Yesterday, after the battle..." I state.

"Yes. The juvenile had showed up again and was playing with your daughter. I think Pamela needed a break from the tension of—"

"Must've been fucking adorable." I yank at my hair. "And you thought 'they'd' be asleep at the switch?" Now it's my turn for air quotes. "You realize that little email didn't get anywhere *near* Temple Grandin's inbox. I'm actually surprised it took them so long to get here."

Standing in the doorway, I watch Commander Eminent Domain duck out of the chopper. This time, he's got a friend with him, a small woman in casual civilian clothing—frumpy scientist type. The rotors are still spinning so they have to hunch across the yard.

"What took you so long?"

"You were warned, Mr. Manchester." He stands at the foot of my porch steps, hands on hips, squinting up at me. "Couldn't leave well enough alone, could you?"

"So have we arrived at PHASE TWO now, I guess."

"Good guess." Behind them, soldiers are deploying a ramp down from the back end of their massive craft.

I shut the front door behind me. "What are you going to do?" I ask from the porch. The rotors have powered down somewhat.

"It's known as ground-penetrating radar," the scientist type chimes in, adjusting a Minnesota Twins baseball cap. "Pretty straightforward technology, sir, invented in the late 1970s. It revolutionized our efforts in the beginning."

"Your...efforts?"

A gunmetal-gray all-terrain vehicle exits the chopper and proceeds smartly down the ramp. Through the row of windows, I can see several more waiting inside, and personnel ready to drive them.

"This radar system maps subterranean structures. Overnight, we used a satellite to derive the general layout, the blueprint."

The commander sneers, "That is what *took us so long*, Mr. Manchester."

The ATV traverses the lawn, steered by a young soldier with acne, who nods at me like a supermarket check-out clerk.

The commander continues, "At this particular point in time, we will begin surveying at ground level for the finer details, to locate entrances and exits. These vehicles are mobile radar stations."

The woman points down at my flagstone walkway. "It's where they hide out, sir. It's where they *live*. We learned this long ago. Wherever they're frequently seen or heard above ground, you'll find their dens and tunnels directly beneath."

Beside her, her colleague is positively beaming, as though he himself discovered this secret. "Whenever some fool yells 'fire!' in a crowded movie theater," he informs me, "that's where we move in." He spreads his arms out grandly. "Our nation, Mr. Manchester, is a crowded movie theater."

"Here and there," the scientist type elaborates, "we prune back their numbers, hoping for...well, zero population growth." She indicates the belly of the chopper, and I notice large silver canisters strapped there.

I ask the commander, "Is this your idea of 'peacekeeping troops'?"

"Figure of speech, utilized during PHASE ONE. Next, we infiltrate their forest, make a lot of noise, and then, once they retreat, we go ahead and finish the job. We basically piss down their hidey-holes."

"And what is the piss?"

"I hope you haven't gotten attached to any of these critters, Mr. Manchester," says the woman. "You'd be surprised how many folks do."

"What's the piss?"

"At this time," the commander declares, "for your own safety, we advise you and the others to decamp. Take a vacation."

I laugh painfully.

"We'll be releasing the agent underground, and it's heavier than air so its sinks. But it's very potent stuff and sometimes there *is* leakage. Who knows how close to this house some of their tunnels run?"

"In other words, sir," the scientist type clarifies, "we urge you not to delay, as our technicians certainly will not, once they pinpoint and access the points of entry."

"What. Is. The. Fucking. *PISS*!?" My eyes snap back to the canisters.

"Chlorine gas," the commander brags, "straight out of WWI. Real old-school trench warfare."

Knees buckling, I grab onto the railing. Over my shoulder, Helen stands at the window, face stiff, knowing better than to come outside, or even to listen at the door.

The rotors are powering back up.

"And here's the beauty part," he shouts, "we don't even have to collect the stinking carcasses afterwards. Way we see it, they dug their own tombs long before our Founding Fathers gave us this land. Not our fault. Repeat: Not...our...fault. We're just making the best of a tricky situation. Maintaining control of God's country."

He bobs on the balls of his feet while I stare down at him and stare down at him and stare down at him. Only his sidekick knows what I mean—she's averting her eyes. But she doesn't have to say a thing, a thing like...*we I forgot about your daughter.*

As the helicopter lifts above us, they hop aboard the ATV and head past the goat-house, into the woods.

What lands in the field?! What lands in the field?!
Is this the little helicopter's daddy looking for his lost child?
Glad I'm not still holding that propeller blade.
Then, I see this one has a pilot inside. And more soldiers.
My new family ran away from the noise. I'm staying behind just for a minute or two. Safe up the climbing tree.
Here comes another joke! This time, I will try harder to understand.
I can watch the pilot through his open door. Using the controls. I can see his dashboard. Reminds me of watching Great White drive the car. The pilot has lots of different things to do with his hands. Making sure the vehicle lands gently. At the end, he just pushes a lever. I watch his hands and I watch his eyes.
Soon, five little cars go rolling out the back of the helicopter. Carrying soldiers. On YouTube, I've seen clowns riding in cars like those. Silly soldier clowns! What are they up to this time?

To make me giggle even more, they all put on scary Halloween masks, like Darth Vader. I remember the mask in the other joke at the pond. And the fake head. These guys!

Then, they pull silver tanks off the bottom of their helicopter and load them onto the little cars. Very carefully. That's another hint for me. The other joke used silver tanks, too. Before everybody started laughing so hard.

The cars drive in five different directions. They pick their paths into the woods and disappear. How am I supposed to understand the joke now?

After he turns the helicopter off, the pilot just sits there. Drinking from a soda bottle. Did Great White give him a Diet Coke? No, no, it's a Pepsi. Yuck.

Sometimes, he talks on his radio. Because of the Pepsi, I know he'll have to go pee. Twenty minutes later, he holds onto a bar and swings out. Takes a walk to the edge of the field.

Knew it!

I drop off my branch. Run across the field. Sit smack in his warm seat! There's his Pepsi in a holder. There's his gun, lying on the other seat. He couldn't take his radio with him because it's connected to the dashboard. Beeping.

The soldier is peeing onto dead leaves. He will notice me.

It's easy to remember what he did when he was landing. I just need to do the same exact things...backward.

First, I turn the key just like Great White does in the car. The motor starts and the propellers go around and around. I pull up the lever and they go faster.

The soldier is running toward me now. Suddenly, his head dips and so does the circle of trees.

I'm up! I'm up!

"Don't worry," I tell myself. I'm not going to try flying anywhere. "Don't you worry." Except straight up. I just need to see from high up.

I like jokes!

"Don't worry."

Then, I can show the others the picture and maybe they will like it, too. I've never seen them laugh. I don't know if they like jokes but I will find out.

I am higher than the trees. Rising. The helicopter is rocking back and forth till I remember which hand the pilot used to steady it. And how the hand moved.

Exactly the same...

What's that out there? Something flying up next to me.

It's the little green bird! Feeling back for being late. Come to keep me company. Not now, little bird. I'm kind of busy!

It's trying to get close. It's having a terrible time because of the propellers. It keeps getting blown down. Tumbling in the air.

Now I'm high enough to see all I need to see. Luckily, most of the leaves are gone. Thank you, my wind! I spot the first three cars right away. The soldiers are lifting silver tanks onto their shoulders and putting them on the ground.

I look for the bird. It's just a dot against the blue sky. Then, it zooms back toward my door. Full speed. I can't raise my arm to protect my head. The bird hits the floor next to me, *thud*.

"Okay, you rest there."

I turn the helicopter a little bit till I can see all five cars below me. These soldier are putting the silver tanks on the ground, too. One of them even sticks a tank *into* the ground. Through a hole.

Oh! I get it! I get the joke! Hahahahaha! Great copying!

They are being my ants, carrying eggs to their tunnels.

Great copying! What a joke!

I make a really bad landing. Almost tip over.

Then, I jump out and start running. The pilot's trying to catch me. "Young lady!" But I'm pretty fast. I've been practicing. "You are in big trouble, young lady!"

I remember the little green bird, so I have to circle back and grab it. Tuck it in my quilt shirt.

Then, I get down on all fours like Funnybone and head for

the forest. Zigzagging like she does. My rhubarb shoes fly off.
　The pilot is right behind me. Now he has his gun.
　That's when everything in the world changes.
　Out from behind a tree steps the father.
　He blocks the sun. I wave up at him. Shyly.
　"Holy...Mother...of...God," says the pilot.
　I hear his gun go *ka......chunk.*
　The father fills his chest with air and knocks me down with an invisible wall of sound. I crawl through the leaves. Tell myself to just keep breathing. I feel like throwing up. Just keep breathing.
　When I arrive at a tree trunk, I lean against it. I can see the pilot trying to breathe too. He drops his gun. Falls to one knee. Like the sick policeman in the valley.
　I bounce. Bounce again. It's the father's footsteps shaking the earth.
　I crawl after him into the woods. Down a trail. Now I'm on all fours but not like before. Hands and *knees*. Too weak to stand.
　Buzz buzz buzz. It is the green bird inside my shirt. Trying to flap its quick wings. Be still!
　I can't keep up. One of the little cars is coming.
　I roll off the trail. Go into my ball between two trees.
　The father crouches behind me. The car is almost here.
　Buzz buzz buzz. Shhhhhhh!
　A thick curtain of hair lowers over me. Dark and smelly.
　The little car zooms right past.
　The father is walking again.
　I can hear the other cars arriving in the field. Soldiers' voices. They sure went to a lot of trouble for that joke. But now they will leave.
　The father and I are heading back to the high room. I can walk now. Down inside, we will join the others and be safe. There is a pile of fresh apples in there. I made a pile of wild leeks in there, too. And some crickets. For water, there is a tunnel to the low

room. That's what we do for water. We drink from the pond whenever we want to. In the high room, we will be okay again.

No. When we get to top of the valley wall, we have to hide again. We can't go any farther. In ferns, we lie on our bellies.

One of the little cars is here. Parked right in our way.

I saw it from the helicopter. Why isn't it gone yet? Your joke is done. Still here?

Three soldiers are watching something through their Halloween masks. Protecting themselves behind their car. Pointing their guns in that direction.

Buzz buzz buzz.

I see what they see. Crawling through fallen leaves. Making a trail through them.

It is Sandy.

He has a dead turkey in his hand. Dragging it by its feet. He is wheezing. Coughing. Gasping for breath. Did he get hurt in the fight? Did the father punish him? I knew it!

There is white foam coming from his mouth. Bubbling out. Some, he spits.

Maybe the father punched him in the belly.

Sandy is crawling right toward us.

Why does he smell like the city pool?

The guns follow him along. What are we going to do when he gets too close? He is crawling more and more slowly. His knees kick out sideways. Foam blows off his lips. His wheezing sounds like a handsaw.

The father stands up. The soldiers see him and freeze. Forget they have guns. Before they remember, he fills his chest and sends out his strongest wave. Luckily, I'm not in the way this time.

They all bend over. I can tell they want to throw up. They support themselves on their car.

Buzz buzz buzz. Quiet, quiet, little bird!

The glass on one of their Halloween masks suddenly cracks.

A rock. Good shot, Funnybone! There she is. She threw a rock from the top of the valley. Rantea-Took is standing beside her. She does a back-flip. Another.

Then, she notices her brother looking at something. She looks, too.

Sandy is lying on his back now. Choking on that foam. His hands at his throat. His eyes are looking around. Like they can find air to breathe over there. Or over there.

The turkey is a bundle at his side. My wind flicks its light feathers.

The soldiers are feeling better. Shaking their heads. Checking their guns. A radio crackles with a man's voice. "Neutralize the one down, load and retrieve. Repeat: Load…and…retrieve."

Good luck *loading* Sandy. He is twice as big as your little car!

"Do not shoot others."

They will not shoot us.

"Deliver the package and withdraw. Repeat: Deliver…package…and…withdraw."

We are getting a package. A reward? Because I figured out the joke?

The father steps away, arms swinging with knowing what to do next. I'll bet he is going to gather good plants to make Sandy feel better. Maybe he feels guilty for punching him in the belly way too hard.

We follow him over the top of the valley. The soldiers are talking behind us.

On the slope, we pass three silver tanks they must have dropped. When Sandy came crawling?

The father lifts the cork-rock out. He will get us safe first, then worry about Sandy.

We all climb down into the high room.

He pulls the rock back into place.

The mother is in here. Her children return to her through rays of sun.

Above us, the soldiers' voices are strong again. They are working at the cork-rock. Package for us.

The father is just sitting in a corner by himself. Hunched over with his head held low.

To cheer him up, I send him a picture of exactly what I saw from the helicopter. He is not paying attention. I send it again. Along with a picture of my ants carrying pale eggs. Back and forth between the two pictures. Such funny copying!

Head held low. I guess they really don't understand jokes like I do.

Suddenly, the whole room fills with sunlight. The rock is out. Everyone looks up at the opening. Here it comes!

Buzz buzz buzz. Okay, okay, okay. I take the green bird out of my shirt. Only one wing is flapping. The other is broken. Around its foot something is tied. A ribbon?

I go hold it inside a ray. A piece of paper, not a ribbon. Words written...

> *POISON GAS!!!!*
> *Get Away!!*

That is Great White's handwriting.

In the wild boy's spot, I mean Rantea-Took's spot, I find the stones he likes to click together. A pile of them. I take just one to the smooth stone wall. Drawing fast. It is not a very complicated picture. Just five Xes in the right spots.

I point to the picture and the father looks. He is looking!

A tank falls through the opening and lands in the dried grass. Hissing.

Funnybone starts coughing. The mother picks her up. Gagging on the air. Like Sandy. My eyes sting. My lungs are heavy.

The father is still staring at my picture. This time, I point to the X that means You Are Here. Then, I point to the floor.

"RAAAHTHUK!" He reaches toward his son.

That's definitely not how I would have pronounced the wild boy's name. Probably, the father knows better than I do. He father leads the way out the main tunnel.

Behind us, two more hissing tanks drop onto the floor.

Raaahthuk gags loudly. Pushes his mother and sister to follow his father.

Nobody pays attention to me. I find a place between father and son. Holding my breath as long as I can. When I have to breathe, I have to cough. My lungs heave.

Red. That's what color the light is in here. Everybody has turned their eyes on. Everybody except me. Will I learn how?

We can't keep going in this direction. This tunnel probably just leads to another X on my map. We can't go there. I saw from the helicopter.

Great jokes can be death, too. Ha ha.

The father knows the map. He takes a sharp left turn into another tunnel. Like a rabbit hole, slanting down.

In some places, he has to stop and dig. The walls are partly collapsed. This tunnel has not been used since when? He squeezes through on his belly so we can follow again.

It gets much steeper till we're scraping downhill on our butts.

The red light starts mixing and mixing with greenish yellow. We reach level ground. The sun is here to greet us. Pouring in through a ceiling of moss and roots. Loose. Like Swiss cheese.

Small animals have taken over. We step through a noisy snowdrift of acorns. Must be years' worth. Squirrels escape between our legs, then jeer at us from above.

We work the holes wider with our hands and poke our heads up into an afternoon pine forest.

Our five heads breathe fresh air. Only four holes. Funnybone shares one with her mother. Arms wrapped around that thick neck.

Hey, the green bird! I still have it in my hand. You need to breathe, too?

We almost died up there.

Raaahthuk's shoulders are bleeding again. All the paste has been scraped off.

Sandy. He was bringing that turkey for *us*.

The chopper thunders overhead, filled with the cast of PHASE TWO, and off past the horizon.

Then, it's a bunker mentality here at the house. Over a fresh bottle of whiskey, we sniff for creeping chemical death while listening in remotely to the long, slow escape beneath the earth.

Thank goodness, the hummingbird's tiny battery lasts just long enough. Even if the video screen is dark—showing the inside of Pam's tight fist—the microphone manages to convey the sounds of life.

I get the impression it's like an ant farm down there, and somehow they're avoiding the flow of chlorine gas. The signal fades in and out, but we can generally follow the decrease in coughing and gagging.

We dance and cheer and embrace when Pam's hand cracks open to blue sky and the sharp tips of pine trees. There's a glimpse of Big Daddy sitting on the ground, head and shoulders sagging, exhausted. Then, her fingers close tight again.

The next two days are disturbing, even by recent standards. In the wake of the governmental double-tornado, we're left in a vacuum, groping for meaning or any sense at all of the near future.

Marlene's still terrified to go home, sleeping on the couch and trying to wriggle back into Helen's and my good graces, as though the unlikely fact of Pam's survival, by itself, can reverse this woman's crime of ego.

Meanwhile, the Internet campaign continues against me, and it's getting plenty of traction within the autism community, although FOX 9 News is still beating the loudest drum.

Both Helen and Marlene have urged me to simply take the "Kid Genius!" page down. I guess on some level I must believe I deserve the abuse, though not because I'm "a huckster profiteering off his daughter's handicap."

Well, "profiteering"…guilty. Exploiting her, also true. But a "huckster"? Hardly. I'll add an occasional, plaintive little comment to the discussion thread, pointing out that Pam is everything she appears to be…*and so much more*. To which the TV station replies, "Prove it!" and "We're coming to bust your ass!"

"They will definitely change their tune," Marlene asserts over her plate of barbecued chicken, "once they see Pamela operating a Chinook helicopter!"

"Marlene," I say, "you are stupid." The brief truce and fellow feeling of the bunker has long since given way to pure resentment—I need this woman gone.

We've revived the military fire pit in the back yard so that we don't have to share a confined kitchen space. Helen and I had hot dogs for dinner and now we're using the low flames to warm our hands. They're calling for flurries overnight. Flurries!

"It would show the world what autistic savants are capable of. Funding for research would swell. And really, what can they do to her at this point anymore?"

Helen always gives the same answer, so I don't have to. "The troops would come back, and Pam would be charged with stealing federal property."

Marlene chews reflectively on a drumstick. "If they can find her and detain her, so much the better. At least she'd be out of danger."

"Go home," says Helen.

We've run out of words.

But before long, we hear another type of communication—a soft tapping from the tree line. It's dark, but when I kneel at the kiddie pool and start splashing, Pam's laughter says it all.

Helen adds fresh logs to the fire. As if our daughter will pull up a chair.

Another sound joins in, too, a squeaking or squealing that I've heard before only through the remote microphone—the juvenile girl!

My wife's patience runs out. Her attempts to approach them across the yard are met with prolonged silences.

Marlene retrieves her tablet from the house. Instead of making the same mistake as Helen, the expert psychologist sits down and bathes her face in the glow of the screen, checking her email, stubbornly *paying no attention* to the visitors. She whispers to us, "The idea is to generate interest by minding one's own business. Soon, they should work their way in closer to us."

They do not.

For my part, I just keep returning to the pool and splashing, which is the one successful method of contact. Once she stops trying to push the envelope, Helen can't get enough of our daughter's contented noises. We even throw charred hot dogs over there and then marvel at the enthusiastic lip-smacking.

By morning, our situation has brightened—aside from a pretty dusting of snow.

The two playmates are still on hand, sharing a thick branch halfway up a tree, and Marlene is nowhere to be seen. *Good riddance.* I heard her car pull out before dawn.

The juvenile is slumbering peacefully, as if on a bed, balanced and insulated, while Pam shivers, miserable, repeatedly walloping herself in the ears to create body heat. With every swing, she nearly falls off.

Why has she come home instead of remaining underground,

where it must be a lot warmer?

I toss an old blanket halfway toward the tree and, when we emerge from the house again after coffee and eggs, we find that Pam has climbed down and wrapped herself in it like a cigar on a layer of dead leaves, blending in, all except for her weary little face.

This reminds me. This reminds me! When I was young, they used to stand on the yard just like this. I would try to make them laugh. I would flip and spin. I'm too old for that now. I have to rest.

Here in Great White's blanket, I finally get warm. I keep falling asleep for a few seconds. I can tell because they have moved a little bit every time. One time, I open my eyes and they're sitting in chairs. Still staring at me.

I do not look at them. At their faces. I look at the baby goat instead. Grown so big! Not a baby anymore. It is afraid to come over. Sniffing the grass. Where is your mother?

I know Great White wrote the note that saved us from the poison gas. I don't know how he got it on the little green bird. I want to make the others understand what he did. But first, I take the bird out of my shirt and toss it near him on the grass. To show him that I know.

It is dead. Even though it's a machine, it's dead now.

Great White picks it up and starts to smile at me. I see the start of the smile. Before he can finish making it, I'm looking back into the woods.

The father, the mother, and Raaahthuk won't come close. They just won't. They aren't too far away, either. Funnybone and

I are the brave ones today!

I roll onto my back and look up. Find her still sleeping on our branch. The sun lights up the very ends of her thick hair. Making an outline like she's wearing tinsel.

This is an even more comfortable position. Lying on my back. I wish I had a snake to eat.

Funnybone crunches an apple. Sitting at my feet. Picks up another apple off the ground. I turn my head and blink at one sitting by my nose. From our apple tree.

The chairs are empty. I slept too long.

I shed the blanket like a skin. While I am peeing behind a tree, I see Raaahthuk squatting on his haunches about a hundred feet away. I am not embarrassed. My pee is steaming. I have seen him pee plenty of times. And poop. It looks like he is pooping now but he is not. He is keeping an eye on his sister and me.

Where are your parents? He flashes me a picture. They are leaning against two sides of a tree.

I finish my apple and start a second. Concentrating on the juice. I am so thirsty.

I hear the screen door slap shut. They have brought some things from my room. My two pillows. My hairbrush. My collection of wild animal posters. My Kindle. They set everything out carefully on the grass. Forgot my piggy bank.

They move their chairs farther away. To give me enough room to love my bedroom things again.

No. Sorry.

Pretty soon, Funnybone is playing with the hairbrush!

They are laughing from their chairs.

She is not brushing her hair. She is banging the hairbrush against the Kindle.

I run on all fours to rescue the Kindle. I use all fours to show them what I am. What I am not. The Kindle feels good in my hands. Old friend. I throw it back at them. Spin it along the grass like a skipping stone.

Then I chase Funnybone. Like we always do. Why do I do it? She is so much faster than me! She pretends she is afraid that I'll catch her. This makes me laugh! We are running on all fours together. We go in circles in the leaves. In and out through tree trunks. I really can't stop laughing!

Funnybone suddenly jumps straight up. Shrieking to show me how high she goes. Back on the ground, she moves slower and slower in front of me. She's letting me catch up. She's letting me! A brand new game! I bet I am supposed to try and tag her.

Right before my fingers can touch, she will show me how slow I am all over again. She will take off like a shot!

But I do tag her. She doesn't gallop away. She plays dead at the edge of my yard. What is she up to now?

Stuck to her back is an orange ball of fluff. I reach for it. It won't come loose. I get a better grip. Out comes a round silver part and a long silver needle.

Great White shot her with sleeping poison? Don't look at him. Don't look. Don't look. Don't look.

The baby goat sniffs her toes. They twitch a little. She is still alive. She is still ticklish.

Remaining on one knee, Sheriff DiMarco lowers her tranquilizer rifle.

Helen moans as if she herself has been hit.

From behind the goat-house, Marlene emerges, standing proudly beside DiMarco. Next come Fiske and Rooney, armed with heavier rifles. Their vehicles must be parked down the road.

Looking grim and determined, the two men rapidly cover the distance to the body in that crouched law-enforcement crab-step.

Though Fiske and Rooney don't point their weapons at me—only wag the muzzles in this direction—my arms rise reflexively.

Pam is already back up the tree, this time climbing higher than before. She's left the blanket down below, but I'm glad to notice that the sun is strong up there, where leaves are few.

Fiske and Rooney begin tugging the juvenile across the lawn, feet first. Marlene tracks their progress with her cell phone.

I scan the forest—*C'mon...c'mon...where are you?*

DiMarco loads another dart. She won't make eye contact with me.

Marlene will.

I shout, "You are a nightmare."

"*You*, Jim, are stupid. Do I really need to remind you that you are still in breach of Minnesota State child welfare regulations? Nothing has changed."

"That's why you are *remanding* this wild animal and not the poor victimized human child?"

"One step at a time. All part of the plan," she explains, pushing open the goat-house door and shooing out the occupants, who bleat furiously.

C'mon...c'mon...c'mon...

It's not until Fiske and Rooney have dragged the limp girl halfway across the threshold that reinforcements arrive—Big Daddy and his son, rising from behind the fallen tree. In this context, I can finally judge size. The tree comes up to Big Daddy's knees, his son's waist, and as I recall...my shoulder.

He has just begun filling his chest with air when the shots go off.

Fiske aims over their heads. Not Rooney. He hits the man in the hand, badly damaging two fingers. The son ducks out of sight as his father backpedals fast, breaking branches, hand stuck in mouth.

Helen and I grab hold of each other. She sharply weeps onto my shoulder. I press my cheekbone down against her skull, trying to feel intense physical pain.

Once the girl has been deposited inside the structure, DiMarco directs Rooney to lean against the door. Then, she sprints off down the road, still armed.

Rifles cocked, Fiske and Rooney check behind the fallen tree. The smaller male must have crawled away.

The shiny white squad car skids to a slanted halt in gravel. DiMarco has brought power tools and proceeds to install an industrial-gauge lock on the goat-house door, complete with a keypad and a thick metal cross-bar worthy of a bank vault.

I take my smartphone from my pocket and stare at it. Should I risk everything? My daughter is now wailing, barely clothed, at the top of the tree. Her best friend might be dying of respiratory paralysis. What are the pros and cons here exactly?

"Ha ha! You should see your *face*, Jim! Feeling indecisive? You were so happy to rub my nose in this inconvenient truth again and again, right? All our devices are locked into *their* grid. Use any of them to contact the outside world and bam, that chopper will darken this sky again before you can turn around."

She has us there. Of course.

Marlene gives the screw a last quarter-turn. "And none of us wants to find out what PHASE THREE is."

So this is what a straitjacket feels like.

Helen bumps my hand. I understand she's signaling me, and I understand she's smart. Nevertheless, I'm annoyed. The second bump does the trick, though. My fingers close around something slick.

Pam's Kindle.

"This is Pepper Vance, reporting live from an undisclosed location outside of St. Cloud, Minnesota."

Helen and I are huddled in the living room, watching it all play out on TV, avoiding yet another circus on the lawn. At least this time it's only a *media* circus. To their everlasting credit,

FOX 9 News got here less than an hour after I wrote them on the Kindle with a dare and directions—"James and Pamela Manchester are ready to go on the air...but it has to be *right now!*"

Unfortunately, we have been aggressively pre-empted.

"I'm here with quite a notorious character, Marlene Stevens, known far and wide through her controversial appearance on Jimmy Fallon's TV show. Frankly, Marlene Stevens, we didn't expect to find *you* here, of all people, in the middle of nowhere! The Bigfoot Hoaxer herself. But I guess it makes a weird kind of sense, being that tomorrow is Halloween."

"Well, Pepper," says our old therapist, "believe it or not I was delighted to see you and your satellite truck, because I actually have something to show you. And the *world.*"

DiMarco enters a long series of numbers on the keypad, not visible from this angle. She raises the cross-bar and swings open the goat-house door. Nothing but darkness inside this windowless space until a crew member fetches a floodlight from the truck and then reveals the captive. The furry girl is rocking back and forth in the corner.

The camera zooms in.

Marlene's voice—"Pepper, what you see here is a juvenile Bigfoot, female, captured this morning on this property. You see, the whole thing was never a hoax. My video at the pond was 100% real. What you saw there was the alpha male, and this is his very young daughter. There is a *family* of these primates living in the immediate vicinity. We will soon be allowing access by scientists, who will examine our specimen and verify precisely what we have."

The reporter's voice—"Yes, yes. I hear you, Bruce. Wait, say again? Okay, everyone. Everyone, *everybody*, listen! We're going national. Got it? National feed in ten...nine...eight...."

The cameraman stumbles into the goat-house, followed by the floodlight operator, who holds the light close. This causes the juvenile to cover her eyes, straining to lift her still-heavy arm.

I might puke up my breakfast.

Marlene appears in frame again, crawling on the wood floor and then kneeling beside her trophy, patting it on top of the head, grinning out at America.

Helen rushes down the hall to the bathroom, where she *does* vomit.

Out on the lawn, I fight my way to the goat-house, flinging FOX employees aside, including Pepper Vance, who drops her microphone.

Once inside, I'm even less gentle in extracting the cameraman, the floodlight operator—and Marlene's arm? I nearly wrench it out of its socket.

I slam the door. "This is *my* property. Sheriff DiMarco, please."

Before re-engaging the lock, DiMarco gets the okay from Marlene, who is busy restoring her blood flow.

"Well, well, well…Mr. *Manchester*, I presume." Pepper Vance has retrieved her microphone and partially straightened her hair. The cameraman is a pro, too, already locked back onto her.

The reporter holds my elbow. "Mr. *James* Manchester. For viewers across the country, this man has been making quite a name for himself here in Minnesota. With questions swirling around his treatment of his severely autistic daughter. We'll get to that, but first, sir, would you mind telling us how you connect with the creature inside this shack?"

Finally on TV…and I freeze. The cameraman offers me an encouraging hand gesture—relax and breathe.

To collect my wits, I take a look around. Pam's still up the tree, keeping herself nice and quiet, just watching the whole scene unfold below her. Nobody else has noticed her yet.

Nobody except for Helen, who stands on the front porch, clutching the Kindle to her chest for moral support.

Where are the…others? It seems funny to call them *Bigfoot* anymore. What should I call them? They're not apes. I replay

Rooney's shooting several times.

And ah look, what have we here? Speaking of apes. Off by himself, behind the satellite truck, if it isn't Commander Eminent Domain himself. So you even monitor local network affiliates? He's in civilian clothes, including sunglasses and the Minnesota Twins baseball cap. The young goat nibbles at his shoes.

How's this for PHASE THREE, sir?

I nod toward the satellite truck.

My turn now, I guess. National feed, millions watching. A new military invasion would be kind of awkward, huh? At this particular point in time.

He slides off his glasses and squints at me, which I find oddly and suddenly relaxing.

"Actually, Pepper, no. Nope. Here's what's going to happen instead."

She kind of laughs at me.

"We are going to show you a little demonstration. Sheriff DiMarco, I've got a question for you."

She's startled when the cameraman locates her. DiMarco gingerly places her tranquilizer rifle down on the grass. "Uh, yes?"

"Does anyone besides you know the combination to this lock?"

"No, Mr. Manchester."

"Not even your two colleagues here?"

Rooney and Fiske look at each other.

"That's right. In fact, nobody in the world knows it but me." DiMarco is warming to the attention. "See, it gets reprogrammed every time. I've got the new combination written down." She withdraws a folded sheet of paper from her pocket. "But I don't need this. It's all up here."

After tapping her temple, she tears the paper into strips.

I should take you on the road.

Suddenly—a series of thuds from the inside of the goat-house wall.

"All right, then. So here's the question, Sheriff. Will you, here before a national audience, will you agree to allow the prisoner to go free if my daughter, Pamela Manchester, is able to open the door?" Pause. "Well, can you think of any reason *not* to take this deal?"

Nothing dawns on DiMarco.

"Wait, wait, now wait." Marlene shoves in beside the sheriff, reclaiming center stage. "Be very careful here. Extremely careful, people. This girl is an autistic *savant*. Do any of you comprehend what that means? That means her brain is not wired the same as ours. On the one hand, Pepper, you have the neurotypical brain, while on the oth—"

"Hey," I bark, "tell it to Fallon."

Laughter from the crew.

She glares at me, of course.

"But where is she, Doctor Stevens?" asks Pepper Vance.

Marlene is forced to shrug. "She must be around here somewhere. You need to grasp the nature of...well, of *cognition*."

I point to the treetop. Everybody follows my finger.

It's a striking image all right—my daughter perched way up there, pale and exposed, pushing the heels of her hands into her eyes—and they all react accordingly. I can hear that the cameraman's throat is tight. As he zooms in, he makes small grunts of emotional satisfaction.

"Good. Great. Now back on me," Pepper Vance calls to him. "Carl." The cameraman's name is Carl. "Carl! Back *here*." Still standing beside me, she regains control, smoothing her stylish pantsuit. "So, James Manchester, is this just another one of your *tricks*?"

More thuds from inside the goat-house, getting stronger. And from off in the woods, someone knocks back. Too subtle for anyone but me to notice—me and Pam, who scans the trees from her height.

"There is no way it could be a trick. Sheriff?"

DiMarco draws a deep breath. "There is no way it could be."

"No, no, no, but you're not listening to me." Marlene gives it one last shot, stamping her feet like one of her own wingnut clients. "Pamela's perceptions are far more acute than—"

"From *that* distance, Doctor?" laughs Pepper Vance, pointing to Pam's perch. "She's going to see the numbers on this lock? Honestly?"

"It must be two hundred feet," says the floodlight operator. "At *least*."

"Let's *go* for it!" The cameraman embarrasses himself with the outburst.

Pepper Vance project her voice. "Okay, folks, *folks*. We need plenty of room. People, please back away from the shack." She organizes the shot—me in the foreground, Pam's tree seen over my shoulder.

"And officers," she adds, "will you kindly put down your weapons?"

Fiske and Rooney reluctantly comply, shaking their heads.

"But really…I have important plans for the subject." I doubt the FOX microphone picks up Marlene's dwindling words. "I'm sure I can teach her to socialize much more effectively than Goodall was able to elicit from her…"

I make a megaphone with my hands. "Pam, Honey, please come down here and let your friend out."

She refuses to move. The crew shuffles their feet. Pepper Vance has her index finger to her earpiece, listening to the producer back at headquarters. "Yes, Bruce." Will they cut away from the national feed…even from local coverage?

The cameraman has not lost faith yet.

When Pam does move, she has trouble at first, so stiff and cold. It takes her two long minutes to make the trip down, branch by branch. I wonder how many sets of eyeballs are viewing this across North America.

And once back on the ground, she's not at all comfortable with everyone—even merely here on the lawn in person—staring at her in that tattered quilt get-up.

"It's just like one of our shows, Honey," I tell her. "This is today's audience. And listen. I promise it will be the last performance you will need to do...*forever.*"

She looks me directly in the eyes. She looks me directly in the eyes.

And then...well, I don't really need to draw out the suspense, do I?

Of course, she approaches the goat-house and easily enters all nine digits in the proper order, then heaves up the cross-bar and swings open the door.

The onlookers can't believe their eyes—*yawn.*

Our neighbor girl must be afraid to escape, so Pam slips inside to help her.

"Pepper, I have a confession to make." She leans the microphone my way. "This is a hoax. This is not real. Fake."

"Wrong! No you don't!" Marlene explodes from the sidelines. "Not true!"

"Fakety-fake-fake."

"Jim, you can be famous," she whispers. "I'll share the glory with you. Don't do this."

"It's already done, Doctor. This is not a Bigfoot. Ironically, I was telling the truth about my daughter and her gifts, but not about this. There are no Bigfoots here...or anywhere else, for that matter. President Clinton was right on target."

"Listen, I'll get you on the 'Tonight Show'." Marlene is in full voice again, vice-gripping my forearm. "Jimmy's people have already been after me to come back on...to explain myself. I'll bring you on with me. *Think* of it. We can blow this whole thing wide open, you and me together."

She actually gets down on her knees. The crew's laughing at her, the camera drinking in the display. Yet, I can tell she is not begging—she's only enhancing her fierce leverage on my ulna and radius, striving for a fracture.

Until the two girls emerge from the goat-house, mine coming out second.

Marlene stands back up.

Helen joins me, relieving her of my arm.

Together on the lawn, together with the world, we all watch this jet-black, furry child, wobbly and insignificant, crossing the yard like on all fours, making for the tree line. She's trying to zigzag, but sluggish, she labors along, legs and arms behaving like rubber, and it's really dreadful not to see the same fluid speed we witnessed for so many hours through the hummingbird cam.

Also on hands and feet, Pam catches up swiftly, then matches her stride for stride. The tomboy has been getting ready for this moment all her life, it turns out.

Better make the most of it myself.

Marlene dashes two or three steps after them, then whirls toward me again. "What we need to do is to think clearly, Jim. *Jim*. Recapture the specimen and have her verified, that's all. It only takes one to rule the world. Don't throw this chance away. Get on board and we'll be famous together. Fiske, Rooney, pick up your weapons."

As if she is somehow their superior, they obey.

The two girls have almost reached the forest.

There is no decision for me to make.

"As you can plainly see, Pepper, that is merely a young human being in a costume, not moving like a wild animal at all. Not moving any better than my daughter. It's a friend from down the road. Melissa. It's just Melissa. This has been a *prank* for you out there, America! Happy Halloween! And Doctor Stevens was part of it from the beginning. Marlene, given your recent track record, that pathetic pond hoax, I'd hate for you to post your cell phone footage from this morning...our neighbor girl being darted and hauled into custody."

Marlene screams, "Fiske, Rooney…fire!"

"Marlene, let me." DiMarco aims her tranquilizer rifle.

"Too late for that, Sheriff."

The two riflemen sight the target through their scopes.

I believe this is the correct sequence of events.

First, Marlene's voice rings out from somewhere inside the forest—"Fiske…Rooney! FiskeRooney!" Oh, it's her voice precisely, though her lips didn't move, and she's not suddenly teleported into the woods.

She's thinking, *Echolalia.*

The news crew is thinking, *What the fuck?* Everyone's trying to locate the source.

Fiske and Rooney have lost concentration.

Second, a rock strikes Rooney right between the shoulder blades, causing his weapon to leap out of his hands. Everyone wants to locate *this* source now, with no better luck.

Third, Fiske receives a blow to the groin and takes a dive. An apple rolls away. That was a hundred-foot bullseye! Pam's celebrating, wildly flapping her hands at the apple tree.

Fourth, I catch the culprit, Frick, ducking back behind the squad car. I recognize him by his auburn conehead. He's now peering through the windows on both sides, far and near. No one else has spotted him yet.

Fifth, another call rises way off in the trees, but this time from another direction entirely, behind my house. It's Pepper Vance's voice—"Carl! Back *here.* Carl! Carl! Carl!" Camera on his shoulder, he swivels toward the disembodied command, but then, seeing his reporter before him in the flesh, still ten feet away, he just shakes his head and continues panning the area for a more available subject.

Sixth, before he can locate and film the rock-thrower, I tackle Carl to the turf.

Seventh, from his peripheral post, Commander Eminent

Domain flashes me a thumbs-up. I use a different finger, and then he retreats at a trot down the road. The young goat bounces after him for a while before turning back home.

For good measure—eighth—Pam plucks another hanging apple, cocks her arm, and lets fly once again, hitting Marlene square in the forehead.

Go, Funnybone!
Good shot, Raaahthuk! Good shot!

After the noisy people drive away, we have time to rest. I drink lots of Diet Coke. Great White did not poison Funnybone. He will not poison me, either.

But he sure does annoy me. Holds the Kindle out for me to see. "Little Ticket," he says, "Little Ticket, look—we're *trending*!"

Whatever that means.

We don't dare acknowledge what Pam is doing.

We just stand here casually on the lawn, chatting about how to hire a lawyer on no money, the bleak season ahead for the Minnesota Timberwolves, and children who have become wild throughout history.

Pam is leaning against Helen's legs.

I guess I will stay here for a while. I can always go back.

Far away through the trees, the mother is gathering good plants.

Funnybone does flips beside her.

clickclickclick

Hilarious. So hilarious!